Amasa A. Marks

Marks' Patent Artificial Limbs

with India rubber hands and feet

Amasa A. Marks

Marks' Patent Artificial Limbs
with India rubber hands and feet

ISBN/EAN: 9783337223892

Printed in Europe, USA, Canada, Australia, Japan

Cover: Foto ©Andreas Hilbeck / pixelio.de

More available books at **www.hansebooks.com**

MARKS'

PATENT

Artificial Limbs,

WITH

INDIA RUBBER HANDS AND FEET.

Office and Manufactory,

575 BROADWAY,

New York City.

Directly opposite the Metropolitan Hotel.

NEW YORK:

N. F. TURNER, STEAM BOOK AND JOB PRINTER,

163 Mercer Street.

1876.

CONTENTS.

PREFACE.

In presenting this work to the public, or that portion of it interested in its contents and the subject it is intended to illustrate, it seems to call for a few remarks under this heading.

Being mindful of the progress in inventions generally at this period of advancement in our nation's career, and knowing, by an extended experience, of the increasing needs in this branch of artistic and mechanical labor, it seems proper to remind my readers and patrons (who do not know by perusal) that this edition is a revision, in part, of several editions heretofore published, together with additional matter pertaining to this important subject; and it seems appropriate, in this CENTENNIAL YEAR, to thus revise, enlarge and set forth such points of improvement as interest our patrons, in order to mutually benefit us all.

I therefor ask you in all kindness to read and consider fairly the contents of this work in its bearings upon the subject which it aims to instruct and illustrate. The work must speak for itself; and here allow me to return my grateful thanks to all those who have so liberally contributed to its pages, with such experimental facts as not only to interest, but inform the reader with such evidence as to make complete, in every particular, the simple object of this work.

A. A. MARKS.

INTRODUCTORY.

Twenty-three years of arduous, purplexing, anxious, thoughtful and almost incessant labor brings me to this period in a calling, of its importance, dignity and benefits to mutilated humanity, of which others can better speak than myself. It has brought me in contact with ALL the grades of human life and made me a listener to a thousand tales of suffering and distress, sometimes of such a painful nature that my anxiety was only for the end of the story. The old man of seventy years has told me how he lost his leg by his horses taking fright from a stone rolling down the bank, and running away, tearing the carriage to pieces, wounding him in several places, and breaking his leg *all to pieces*, as he bluntly describes it. The result was amputation above the knee.

Others in middle life, too numerous to particularize here, tell the varied histories of their loss ; some, *yes many*, in Battle, and many by the most trifling accidents ; but those touching my sympathies most tenderly are the children's stories ; one in particular comes up in my mind at the present moment : it was a little, rather frail boy of less than ten years ; his father was a farmer, and was drawing logs ; the boy was following behind the oxen when they were drawing only the loose log chain, with its long hook dangling at the end : by some means it caught the boy's ankle, and after dragging him for a short distance by the leg. the chain ran through between two stumps, very close together ; the result was it took the little fellow's foot completely off at the ankle.

The little girl has told me how, when crossing the street in this great, noisy city, she was knocked down by a hack, the wheels passing over her little leg, and crushing it so badly that there was no way of saving her life but by amputation of the mangled leg.

It would make a great, yes, an immense book, to contain the many tales of suffering to which I have listened. You read them in the newspapers every day, and interesting and thrilling as they read there, they are by no means so painfully exciting as when told by the person most interested. It would seem as if this calling was one continuous scene of misery ; yet, looking back these many long years, I find it has not all been an experience of a sorrowful character.

Maimed and mutilated persons are by no means the most miserable or unhappy, as most people are likely to think. There are some who take their losses sorely at heart, and mourn year after year over them as if they were suffering untold agony, and constantly relating their maimed condition all through life. But they are very few in proportion to the large army of jovial and happy ones, and take them as a body, they are unquestionably full as cheerful as the average run of mankind, many frequently expressing themselves that they are *very thankful, that it is no worse.*

The young miss and the young lad, as well as those in middle life and even old age, who "sport" their artificial limbs unknown to the world, are usually cheerful, and enjoy life and jokes to a remarkable degree. I have frequently heard them tell about persons treading upon their (*artificial*) toes, and begging their pardon without knowing anything obout it until the "beg pardon" was uttered by the trespasser, in supplicating tones. But, strange as it may seem, the happiest and most jolly set of fellows I have ever come in contact with is a company of maimed soldiers, especially when those from the far distant parts of the country meet by accident, and talk over their former trials, and, as it were, "*fight their battles over again.*" You do not witness much crying and whimpering there among a dozen or more who sometimes meet in my office ; they very soon get acquainted, and are almost sure to know something of each others' history in the war, and have some great event of their own to relate—this applies as well to one army as to the other. I have often listened to soldiers of the North and of the South, who had met for the first time, to their own knowledge, but upon talking over old matters and giving an account of their escapes, *and what were not* always just exactly *escapes*, they found they were not far apart when the bullets whistled by, *and not always by, either*, but could relate trivial and sometimes important incidents that the one knew of as well as the other ; they would tell how their own side were "licked" and the other side didn't know it, and *vice versa*, and so on. But pardon this digression from my subject.

I started to write on Artificial Limbs, without intention of discussing or relating the prior causes or events calling into use the products of my labor ; but whether opportune or not, it may be interesting to some, and if it should dispel the gloom of but few persons who entertain these melancholy thoughts that they are the most *unfortunate ones* in the world, then this brief, historical introduction will not be without accomplishing some good.

TO ALL WHOM IT MAY CONCERN.

My views of the requirements of an Artificial Leg are: First, *ease* and *comfort* in walking. Second, a natural motion, lightness, elasticity and stillness, combined with a graceful step. Third, reliance, stability, firmness and durability.

In all these respects I claim that my Artificial Legs, with my patented India Rubber Feet, are pre-eminent.

The Legs are, in the first place, made to fit the stump so as to give the greatest ease and comfort to the wearer, while it operates with freedom, firmness and elasticity. Thus all these indispensable objects are attained, without that complicated mass of machinery resorted to in other kinds of Artificial Legs. In fact, there is no *machinery* in them (that is, what is usually called machinery.) This fact makes the leg unequalled in point of durability by any similar invention yet presented to the public.

In giving a description of my inventions it does not require a mass of words, nor a complicated description of them to make the most ordinary mind realize and appreciate their absolute value, and the causes which led me to adopt and develop my inventions. Their various and many advantages over all others now in use, will be apparent when the following facts are fully weighed.

In my opinion, it has been well understood among inventors and manufacturers of Artificial Legs, that there was *something* required to improve the foot and ankle, and give more stability and less unnecessary motion. This was needed to obviate that jerking, clapping, snapping and rattling noise, and unnatural and exceedingly unpleasant sound, both to wearers and others, so frequently heard, and by which Artificial Leg wearers might be heard and observed from other persons at some distance in the street or moving about the house. Some have sought the removal of this difficulty in one way, and some another ; but most inventors have, in trying to avoid the difficulty, but added to it. By multiplying machinery of various kinds, although aiming to get rid of *worse than*

useless motions, they have added complication to complication, by their many cords and springs which have a tendency
to please the unexperienced while the limb is new and unused,
but invariably *displeases* them soon as a little wear brings the
trappings to a test, and not only warns the wearer of the in-
stability of his substitute by its many unreliable and *uncon-
trolable* gyrations and unpleasant sounds, but annoys and
startles his neighbor as he passes his quiet door, and alarms
the congregation when he enters the house of Public Worship,
the inventor not stopping to think that every additional cord,
spring, joint or contrivance but increases the difficulties, adds
to the already enormous complications, weakens the limb, and
renders the invention liable to greater objections, without accomplishing any advantages whatever.

In these statements I firmly believe I express the views of
a large number of inventors. At all events, I *know* I give my
own experience, having been engaged in this calling of giving
relief to mutilated sufferers for the last twenty-three years,
and having also been most of my life engaged in mechanical
labors of a nature both instructive and beneficial to one ac-
quiring knowledge of this important art. I feel, therefore,
that my labor has been well bestowed in thus being able to
give to the unfortunate an Artificial Limb accomplishing every
required movement and all the essentials to make the most
life-like, light, easy and durable leg ever given to the public,
while, at the same time it is free from *all* cumbrous machinery,
It is the *ne plus ultra* of Artificial Limbs now in use, as all
impartial examiners have declared.

The India Rubber Foot is the base of the whole structure,
and, although it is elastic, springy and light, it is also the
most *riliable, firm* and *substantial* foundation that ever a
poor limbless person stood or walked upon. This I assert
without fear of successful contradiction.

When I first invented and applied my Rubber Feet to the
Artificial Legs, I did not think they would be suitable for the
delicate and fastidious. It was intended more especially for
the hard-working mechanics, the farmer, and those whose
lives demand toil, energy and constant exertion. But in this
I was most agreeably disappointed. To my own surprise and
gratification, I soon found it was equally well adapted to their
wants as to any others'. Nay, more, it was just the thing for
the most tender, delicate and sensitive lady in the land ; and

their joy and gratitude in its use, in being able to perform their many and various duties with facility, ease and symetry of motion, without noise or unpleasant observation, has been expressed to me in a great number of instances—a sentiment always encouraging and fully appreciated by every one engaged in giving relief to human sufferings.

A word to those who have used and are now wearing the old kinds, with the movable, clattering ankle joints : Is not your step in your parlors at times taken for a squeaky, broken-down chair, or a rat or a mouse intruding in some corner of the building? Are you not, while walking in the street, sometimes taken for a wheelbarrow crying for grease ; and does not your step resemble the clatter of an old shoe with the sole loose and too large for the foot? Is it not a gain to get rid of those annoying appendages and to be relieved of the great expense and trouble necessarily attending them?

My patent Rubber Feet most assuredly obviate all these difficulties. I have applied them to a great number of other makers' legs beside my own, many where the legs were new, and more where they were sound, except where the springs or cords were worn out or broken, and have succeeded in making the old leg as good, and, in fact, much better in many cases than a new one of that kind.

I would not state, nor have it inferred from what has been here said, that my leg will last always, under all kinds of rough usage, but this I do say, that it will outlast two of any other kind now in use (that are fit to use), and that when it does need repairs—and what thing earthly will last always?—it will cost less and be always less troublesome than any other Artificial Limb I know of. Its simple mode of construction is conclusive to every one, that one of its important and valuable features is its non-liability of requiring repairs, and its ease of access when repair is needed, thus rendering the expense and trouble comparatively trifling. And now, after a period of over thirteen years of unparalleled prosperity, during which time they have received the most exalted and continued praise throughout this broad land in this branch of invention, *yet*, there is even now, and always will be, an *occasional* RIP VAN WINKLE, just waking up after his *twenty years' sleep ;* and once in a while one turns up who does not really understand my inventions, just because they are so *very* simple. This trouble has arisen from the fact that it has been represented in the theories of the past by those who either did not know or did not want the unfortunate ones to know that there really was any difference between Natural and Artificial Limbs. It was my object in former editions of my pamphlet to have this point clearly understood. If I failed in this point there, I shall endeavor to not do so here, but show that Artificial Limbs *are Artificial Limbs*, and *nothing* else, and all who think they are natural ones, or represent such to be the case, labor under a great mistake, to say the least of it. The human frame is such a wonderful and mysterious construction, that the few skillful artisans who ever attempted to imitate it as a whole by artificial mechanism, for any purpose except as a mere novelty, have utterly failed, and always will fail, as sure as perpetual motion is bound to fail as an invention of man. What I desire to show is that Artificial Limbs are simply mechanical constructions, and made to take the place of lost members of the human body, for the purpose of assistance and appearance, unitedly, for the benefit of persons who have lost such members—they are MECHANICAL CONSTRUCTIONS and nothing else. To what degree they have been made to benefit and assist the unfortunate ones in their journey through life is very well known to the world, and it is not my object here to in any way depreciate the great benefits rendered to mankind by any . and all who have sought to relieve unfortunate humanity by such means as they have deemed proper and best in their own estimation.

Every skilled inventor and engineer who rises to any distinction, always seeks to avoid and do away with everything complicated in their inventions and constructions ; for instance, compare the sewing machine or locomotive of the present day with those made twenty years ago, and mark the difference ; each does ten times the labor now that they did then, and with not one-fourth part of the complications. We all know that the more complicated any mechanical construction, of whatever kind, the more liable it is to derangement and annoyance.

My inventions of 1863 and 1865, after an experience of ten years in following the old theories of making Artificial Limbs with all the cords and flapping ankle-joints, &c., &c., has now become a well settled theory, thoroughly proved by long experience, and not only applicable to Artificial Limbs, but is also practiced to a large extent in surgery ; the ablest surgeons in Germany and other countries, as well as our own, have and are treating cases of disease and injury to the ankle-joint where they cannot maintain the controlment of it, and are compelled, in order to save the foot, to make a passive or laxative motion, that is, such as the patient cannot control at will as formerly ; they treat it in a way to anchylose it, thus making it stiff and without any motion whatever. This system has proved to be far preferable to the flapping and uncertain step necessarily rendered by the old manner of treatment. This discovery in surgery confirms my theories in their fullest sense. I have a large number of such cases of surgical treatment before me, but deem it unnecessary to insert them here, as it has become a well settled system of surgical practice, and proved to be of great benefit to the patient.

HOW I CAME TO INVENT THE RUBBER FEET.

This question has been asked me so *many, many* times, and answered, too, *but only verbally*, that it seems to me to be very pertinent, and I will here give it as brief as possible.

The reader will first impress in his mind that I had been making Artificial Legs for some ten years, after the old styles, with ankle-joints, wooden feet, etc., before the production of the rubber feet. I had, during the last years of this time, become disgusted with this mode of construction of the foot, ankle, etc., and conceived in my mind the idea of a rubber foot, and had spoken of it to others, but could not settle upon a plan of attachment satisfactory to myself, supposing, as I then did, that there *must* be an ankle-joint. There it rested for some time, in a quandary, as it were, until one day an old patient called upon me, who had suffered for some time with a diseased and irritable stump, which was constantly discharging a substance which cut away the tendons and cords of the ankle-joint in a very short time, and consequently *used up the leg.* He asked me, rather bluntly, if I would make him a Leg *all solid* at the ankle, at the same time saying that he could not stand the expense occasioned by his diseased stump. I remarked, Yes ; that could be done by having the heel-cord outside of the leg. He promptly replied, "*I mean, make me a leg without any cords or ankle-joint.*" To which my answer was, "*No. sir ;* it would be of no use to you."

He then argued that he felt sure that I was mistaken, as he had made some experiments in a temporary way that satisfied him that there was really but very little motion required at the ankle. Finally it was agreed that I should make it, and after commencing it on that new idea, and all through its construction, incidents kept coming to my mind of such-and-such of my best operators on Artificial Legs having frequently caused me to tighten up their joints, so as to get but very little motion at the ankle. By the time this leg was finished, applied, and worn a few days, I was satisfied that the rubber foot was all that was needed to make it complete, and at once commenced operations, and soon had them in use, by applying them first to old legs needing repairs, every one of which proved not only satisfactory but so overwhelmingly sought after that the success which has followed is too well known to be even alluded to here.

ECONOMY.

I am fully aware that there are many people in the world like a certain individual who had "drove" an exceedingly close bargain with a shoemaker, to make his boy a pair of shoes for *four shillings*. After the price had been agreed upon, the shoemaker asked: " *What size shall I make them?*" The purchaser answered promptly, "*Make them as large as you can for the four shillings.*" And so it is in this business; some think that the more they get for their money the better off they are. To *those* I wish to say, if they want a music-box, a rattle-box, a rat trap and an artificial leg all in one, and wish to go through the streets with a bell ringing, "*Here I go with an Artificial Leg*," in tones that nobody can mistake, then go where you can be *sure* of getting them, and your *four shillings'* worth too, at that; and when you get tired of that fun come and see me, I won't blame you for making the experiment, neither will I raise my price; it is every one's right to do as they please in matters of their own interest. All I ask is, read this book thoroughly, inquire of those who know from experience, and then act on your own candid judgment.

WEIGHT.

Much is said by the manufacturers of the complicated styles of Artifical Legs, about the Rubber Feet being heavier than the wooden ones, and thereupon they try to make a great ado about it.

The FACTS are these: The Rubber Feet are of themselves a trifle heavier than some kinds of the wooden feet; but bear in mind that the Rubber Feet require no IRON HINGES, BOLTS, CORDS, GLASS BALLS, SCREWS, or *any* of the paraphernalia whatever used in the ankle-jointed trappings, in "hitching" their wooden feet to their legs. This machinery adds weight, as *all* must know.

In many cases where I have removed the wooden feet, and applied my Patent Rubber ones in their places, I have found, by weighing before and after, that the weight of the Limb was reduced from *one* to *six* ounces by the change.

My Patent Artificial Legs, with the India Rubber Feet, weigh from three to six pounds each, depending upon the weight and occupation of the persons who are to wear them, and the Artificial Legs of my patent average to be some lighter and MUCH stronger than those made as above stated, with their *superfluous appendages.*

ANOTHER FEATURE TO BE CONSIDERED.

Among the many advantages gained by the Rubber feet over the Wooden, or hard and non-elastic kinds, which has been omitted, is the great saving in Stockings, as the Rubber feet do *not* wear out Stockings faster than the natural feet, while the Wooden and Hard feet are well known to wear out full ten to the natural feet one, a matter of consideration to *some* persons, if not to *all* who are required to wear Artificial feet.

The following description, with illustrations, is taken "verbatim et literatum," from the *Scientific American* of April 15th, 1865:

ARTIFICIAL LIMBS.

The engravings published herewith represent Artificial
Limbs, which have novel features not heretofore obtained in
them. India rubber is largely used in their construction, the
feet and hands particularly being constructed of this substance.

Fig. 1

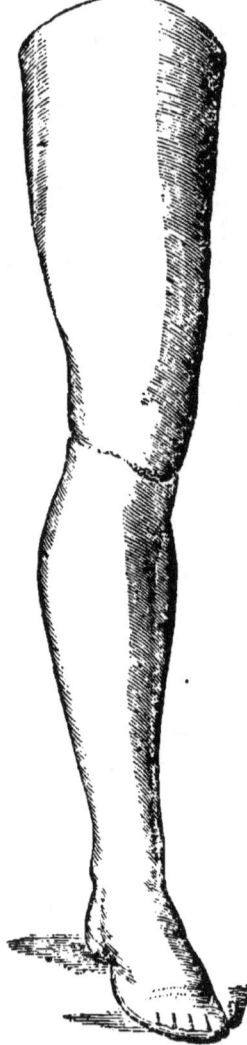

Fig. 1 presents a full-length leg standing erect, to be

applied in all cases where amputation occurs above the knee-joint.

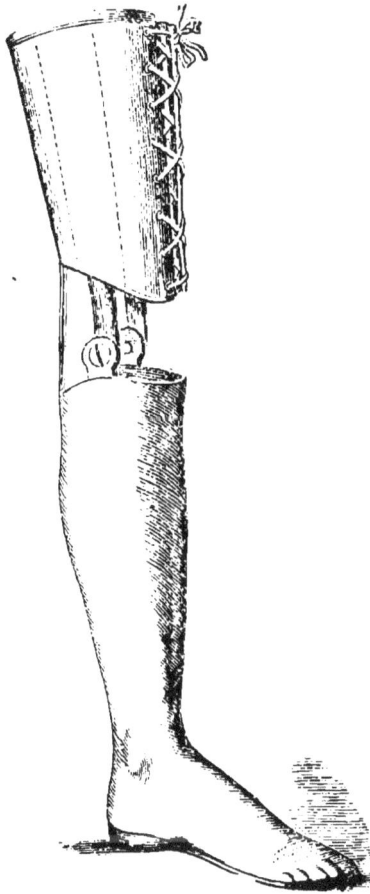

Fig. 2

Fig. 2 represents a leg to be applied where the leg has been amputated below the knee-joint, and the stump is flexible enough and sufficiently long to enable the wearer to use it in walking. It also represents the leg with the heel compressed, and in its position after taking the step, and when firmly planted on the ground.

Fig. 3

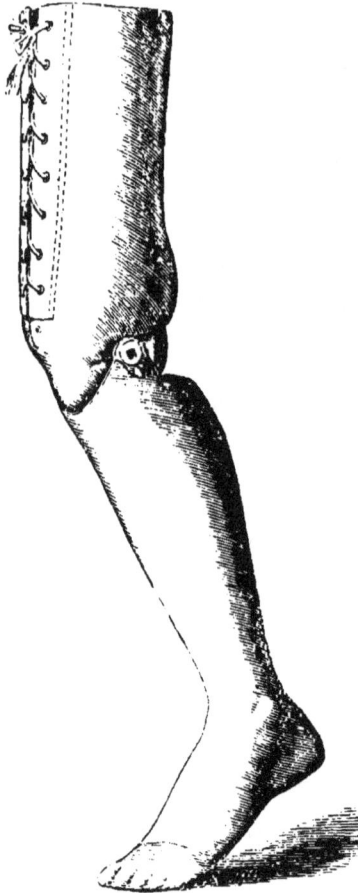

Fig. 3 is termed a knee-bearing leg. It is to be applied where amputation takes place below the knee, and where the stump is too short or contracted at right angles, so the knee-joint cannot be used in walking. This figure represents the leg slightly bent at the knee, and bearing well upon the toe, as in the act of lifting it to take the next advance step.

Fig. 4 is a view of the India-rubber foot before being applied to the leg. This rubber foot constitutes the main feature in the legs shown in the figures. It is made mostly of India-rubber of a very spongy, light and elastic character. A piece

Fig. 4.

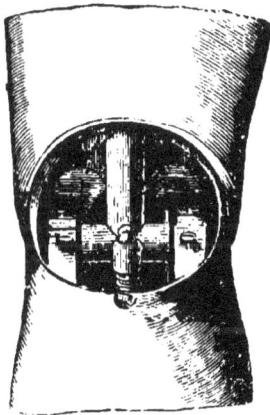

of willow wood, nearly filling the rubber heel at the top, or surface, where the leg rests, runs down about one-fourth of the distance towards the lower part of the heel; also forward and downwards to

Fig. 5.

the joint at the ball of the foot, as shown by the dotted line. This piece of wood is the base upon which the foot is built, and is also the medium whereby the foot is joined firmly to the leg. The leg itself is made of light, tough willow in all cases, except the thigh piece shown in figure 2, and the front part of the thigh piece in figure 3, which are both made of leather. The entire leg and foot in all cases are covered with fine buckskin, neatly coated with a life-like, waterproof finish, making it both light and strong. It will be seen that there are no movable ankle-joints in these limbs, the necessity for which being entirely obviated by the Elastic Rubber Foot, which gives all the motion required in walking, and also the ease, firmness, elasticity and reliance, absolutely necessary in a perfect Artificial Leg.

It would seem at first sight that no one could walk well on any Artificial Leg, without the moving, flapping ankle-joint, but practice proves this to be erroneous.

The Rubber Foot also gives all the required lateral motion to the foot when stepping upon sideling or uneven ground. This leg dispenses with all machinery of whatever character, and has been in use for the last two years, giving great satisfaction.

Figure 5 gives a rear view of the knee joint of the long leg

(Figure 1). The T joint is fastened to the upper part or thigh piece of the leg, and the gudgeons of the T are held in adjustable, oblique boxes, which are easily set at any time by the screws passing through the caps into the main leg, so as to keep the joint to work tight and still, yet free and perfectly flexible, the small projecting bar attached to the T with the button-shaped ball operating upon the spiral spring, so as to throw the foot forward when bent in walking, and so as to hold the foot under when bent at right angles in a sitting position. This feature has been secured by a separate patent, dated March 7, 1865.

Fig. 6.

Figure 6 shows a Rubber Hand, made same as the foot, of which there cannot be as much said as of the other inventions. It corresponds, however, with the others in its characteristic features of simplicity and durability, and wholly dispenses with machinery, giving a softness to the feeling and an elasticity which is very desirable. It is as useful as any hand yet invented, which is not probably saying much in its favor, as no art yet shown, if it ever will, can compare with "nature's handiwork." A patent for this hand has also been obtained, as in fact have all of them, through the Scientific American Patent Agency. These inventions have caused a great change for the better in the appearances, as well as usefulness to those who have lost natural limbs, and must give great relief to the maimed. These inventions, in dispensing with so much machinery, reduce the expenses of repairs very greatly, as there is no complicated gearing to get so often out of order. You see no part of the cuts representing the inside working of the leg, because there is none there to be exhibited, except the lower part of the knee spring, operating as described in Figure 5. The limbs are, of course, hollow in all cases, to render them light, as well as adaptable to covering and supporting the stumps they enclose and sustain.—*Scientific American*, April 15, 1865.

ARMS AND HANDS.

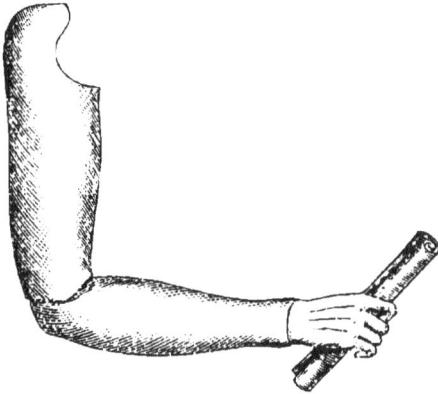

Fig. 7 represents an arm for amputation above elbow. In former editions there has been but little said of the arms and hands, and, in reality, not enough, for their real utility is, in fact, underrated. The soft naturalness and perfect symmetry of the hand is always secured, and no possibility of getting out of repair render them of real service, and are fast taking the place of the wooden and other complicated kinds. It is true you can make artificial hands that perform some feats that my rubber hands cannot, in way of picking up light articles, operated by pulling cords with the opposite arm, and they appear to the uninitiated observer as of great importance; but when you come to subject it to a practical demonstration, you will find that the opposite arm is what does the work, and it might with much more ease do the work itself directly, than to have cords or straps pass over the shoulder to the artificial arm to perform its labor.

Fig. 7.

Cases where both arms or hands are amputated, may be rendered of some practical benefit by these complicated machines; but even then, if you wish to do real work, comply with the old rule—take off your coat, fix for and take right hold of it, and this artificial hand business is no exception to the rule—take out the hand, slip a nice steel, nickle-plated hook in its place, then ten times more real work can be done with it than with all the artificial hands ever invented. The knife or fork is also better used in same way. This change is made by the wearer in a moment, by the aid of a small screw-driver, carried in his pocket, accompanying the arm. The arm is not considered complete without these attachments.

My invention carries with it other important features, such

as cases where parts of hands are amputated ; one, two or more fingers are replaced with rubber ones, to fit and adjust smoothly to the remaining hand, with the best of success and great satisfaction to those requiring them. This is entirely a new feature, and not accomplished by any other process or invention.

Fig. 8.

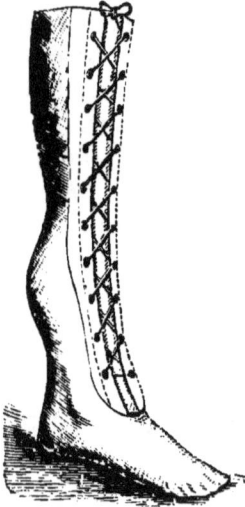

This cut (Fig. 8) represents an apparatus for a deformity such as a shortened leg, generally by hip disease. It encloses the leg and the foot, the latter resting upon the sole, as is usual and proper; it may have an ungainly appearance here, but when dressed there is no apparent formidability, it neatly hides the deformity. I make them, also, with a thigh-piece, for cases where the knee-joint is weak, and support needed above the knee.

The great feature of dispensing with a clattering ankle-joint is particularly important in these cases.

Fig 9.

Fig. 9 represents a short leg, for cases where the leg is amputated at ankle-joint or instep, and where the weight can be taken on end of stump. Such can be applied where the stump is but one and a-half inches shorter than sound leg. For Chopart's operation, a foot has to be made separate, and placed in shoe according to the peculiar shape and condition of the stump.

SAFETY SOCKET.

This is a term given by a manufacturer of Artificial Limbs to what he claims as a new invention, whereby he takes the weight upon the end of the stump.

It would appear from his setting forth of ideas, that it was an entire new discovery in Artificial Limbs. This is by no means the case. I have made them to take the weight on the end, using a pad or cushion for the stump to rest upon, over twenty years ago ; in a large number of cases ever since, and, in fact, *all* knee-bearing stumps take their weight on end or knee, and all other kinds of amputations take a good portion of weight upon the end where they use socks upon their stumps, such as I make and provide in all cases, and have for many years ; but the theory of taking the *entire* weight upon the end of the stump in ALL cases, is in my judgment, founded upon an experience of many years, absolutely preposterous. Those who wish can have them so with no extra charge, and there are occasionally such cases as seem to require such. My object is to treat each case as seems best, and in accordance with the wishes of the patient, after reaching a thorough understanding of the case in question. The word SAFETY is misplaced here, if I know what the word means.

Ask nineteen-twentieths of all the persons who use Artificial Legs, with ordinary amputations (other than knee-bearing), if they can take their entire weight on end of stump? You will not need to wait long for a strong negative answer.

Theory is one thing, practice another, *sometimes*.

AMPUTATIONS.

Some Surgeons will perhaps think it rather presumptious in me to offer any suggestions in regard to the most suitable points for amputation, on the ground that such emergencies necessarily depend upon the circumstances of the case, and they amputate just where they are compelled to, by leaving the stump as long as they can with safety to the Patient and operation, always considering that the longer the stump, the better for the patient, this is generally the true rule to work by, as a long stump is generally preferable to a short one, but they can be too long as well as too short for the benefit of the patient. My experience of twenty-three years in making and applying Artificial Limbs to every form of amputation ever performed in this country, or any other, leads me to prefer the Flap operation generally, and in thigh amputations save all the bone possible, after getting clear from the knee-joint, and room for a good flap. In amputations below the knee-joint, no leg should ever be amputated lower than three inches above the ankle-joint, (for medium sized adult person) and above that point save all that is possible consistent with the case. In cases where a toe or toes are required to be removed, it is undoubtedly best to amputate at the toe joints, or, if necessary, perform what is termed Choparts amputation, but in no cases, from all of the experience I have had in adjusting and witnessed in wearing Artificial Limbs, would I consent to any amputation above this point, save above the ankle-joint at the point mentioned above. Some very important objections to unjointing or amputation about the joints, *either ankle or knee* are ; they are generally a very long time in healing, sometimes never heal at all, and if they do they are extremely tender, a little irritation often causes abscesses and the suffering and trouble attending these afflictions is lamentable, it makes the Artificial Leg cumbersome and large at the joints, with all the inconveniences that must accompany these operations.

These reasons will apply with equal force to arms, except in cases of amputation of the hand, where the wrist joint can be saved, then save all that possibly can be saved below it, as every inch in length or movable part in that important member is of such great value, and every Artificial *Hand* is of so little value that no reasonable comparison can be made between them, and every humane and considerate Surgeon should never fail to preserve all he can of the hand.

How soon after amputation should an Artificial Limb be applied.

To this very important question, which is so frequently asked, I answer : In the first place it depends entirely upon circumstances. Some stumps heal much quicker than others, depending generally upon the condition of the person and cause of amputation. My experience has proved that the most proper time is as soon as the stump is properly healed and the patient recovered from the shock, *before* the stump has become fleshed up, as it is sure to do immediately after this has transpired, this condition is usually reached within six or eight weeks after amputation, and sometimes within a month.

Being aware that patients are quite frequently advised by their surgeon to *not apply an Artificial Limb* until the stump is *strong* and *hard*; such advice, however, emanates from those of very limited practice, observation and consideration, as will be readily seen, for we all know that nothing but use makes the inside of our hands more hard and tough than the outside; nothing but EXERCISE makes and keeps our joints flexible and strong. Allow a sound and healthy arm to hang useless by your side for a single month, and what is the consequence? Every person of good common sense can answer. My long experience and treatment of thousands of cases certainly entitles me to some weight on this subject, and if any person desiring information upon this subject, entertain any doubts as to the correction of my views, then just visit or correspond with some of those who know by *actual experience*, what they have learned, in this matter of serious consequence to all using Artificial Limbs.

CHILDREN

And young persons who loose their limbs befor · obtaining their growth, are generally prevented by the advice of their surgeons or physicians, without due consideration, however, from having Artificial substitutes applied, on the ground that they will out-grow them. This appears at first sight to be a very good reason, but upon giving the subject a little reflection, it will be readily seen, that although the chances are that they are likely in most cases to out-grow them (this article applies more especially to legs) before they are worn out, it is not very well known that they can be lengthened at times, as required, at small expense, and perhaps it is well to here give this bit of valuable information to those interested in such cases, that *these* limbs possess a very important advantage over ALL others in this respect, on account of their being free from the internal complications of cords and springs, which sometimes compose Artificial Limbs, thus saving the largest part of the expense attending the operation of lengthening the limb to keep up with the growth of the patient.

The most important point to be taken into consideration in this matter is, how shall we most benefit the tender sprig of childhood and youth, who meet with these great losses, whether by compelling them to use crutches and grow up round-shouldered, hump-backed, one-sided, or otherwise deformed in some way, as in nine cases out of ten they are from the effects of using crutches, *especially for any length of time*, or, to at once apply a substitute, and pay proper attention to the use of it, and thereby keep them in natural form, and also avoid the very unpleasant sight of crutches to the eye of the parent and public, and the mortifying effect (to say nothing of the great inconvenience) to the patient. Another very important fact should be taken into consideration, which is, that children growing up without a substitute or limb, to exercise their stump, often lose the use of it, either by its becoming contracted or weak for want of use, it is frequently the case that they lose the use of their joints, and can never wear a limb at all, by going without for years, while obtaining their growth, but where the limb is applied at a proper time, and they grow up with it, they never seem to fully realize their loss, and invariably make the most skilful operators in the world. No child that loses a leg at four years of age or upwards, should be allowed to go without a substitute for a single year after the stump is healed, and recovery from the shock of amputation been effected.

Some are without means to secure limbs, and others will say they cannot afford it—then call upon your friends for assistance, or dispense with some of the superfluous ornaments of dress, or do SOME way to provide for the *necessity* of your unfortunate child or friend to avoid its growing up in your sight a constant spectacle of regret, and sorrow to yourself, and thereby remove an almost certain barrier to its proper place in society, and its lasting welfare in mature years.

Having applied Artificial Limbs to children as young as three years, and many at the age of five to ten years and upwards, and always with the best of success (unless where they had been too long upon the crutches), thus obtaining a knowledge not to be mistaken in.—To those who have cases under their care of the nature here mentioned, due consideration to these statements is asked, and although differing as it does from the hasty advice generally given by the physician, weigh well the fact, and your conclusions will unquestionably be right, and your duties plain to those entrusted to your tender care and affection.

The following engravings clearly illustrate the absolute necessity of attention to these matters:

Fig 10.

Fig. 10 represents a little girl, eight years of age, to whom I had applied an Artificial Leg, as there shown, is only one case in many thus treated by myself. The feature of applying Artificial Limbs to children so young is generally considered not practicable by parents, on the ground that they are soon outgrown, costly, and that it's only a child and no matter. It does cost something to apply, lengthen and enlarge as they grow up. Those who think it does not pay, please take this single case in view. This cut is from a photograph taken

Fig. 11.

eight years ago, and that little girl is now 16 years of age. Would she now be as well formed, healthy, and competent to occupy her proper sphere in life, had she grown up without the aid of this substitute? Her picture (Fig. 11), taken September, 1875, shows clearly what she now is.

It is very well understood, that young ladies wearing Artificial Limbs, are not over desirous of having it publicly known: this is not an exceptional case, yet even in this case her name and address will be given, when desired by persons giving satisfactory reasons.

She resides in New York City.

Fig. 12 represents one of the most remarkable cases ever treated, or, at least, that has been reached in my twenty-three years of practice in this line of subsidiary art.

Fig. 12.

His name is THOMAS KEHR, Brooklyn, New York, 10 years of age; was run over by the cars, which caused the amputation of both legs, one above, the other just below the knee. In December, 1875 (just about a year after the accident) I applied a pair of Artificials, as illustrated in this cut. In two weeks thereafter he was walking very well without a cane. Two months passed and he was walking and getting about, up and down stairs, and, in fact, everywhere he wished to go, without any assistance whatever, with such ease and comfort that it was absolutely wonderful for such short stumps as his.

Fig. 13.

The cut (Fig. 13) shows how he appears with his limbs on and dressed. This case is another which practically exemplifies the great importance of applying these substitutes to those who are maimed in tender years.

For a more extended description of this wonderful case, I refer you to the letter of DR. BRADY, on page 35, the attending surgeon, who has taken a deep interest in the lad, and kindly placed the facts in such shape as not only to make it very interesting to all seeking reliable information in these important matters, but at the same time coming as it does from one whose eminence as a skillful surgeon, wise counsellor and respected citizen, and in no way interested except for the welfare of his maimed patients, as a matter of course, bear with it such weight as it rightfully deserves.

First Premiums Awarded with Reports of Judges.

GOLD MEDAL.

Although an inventor and manufacturer of Artificial Limbs for several years, and also an exhibitor at many of the Fairs of the American Institute and other exhibitions of Art, and having received awards of high merits from them before and as late as 1859, a Large Silver Medal from the American Institute, (the last fair held by that Institution until 1865). It is proper to state that those limbs were not of the Improved Patent, which I now make. 1865 was the first year that my limbs with the Patent India Rubber Hands and Feet, and other patented improvements were placed on exhibition in competition for a premium.

A Gold Medal was offered by the Board of Managers as the award for the BEST Artificial Limbs. This great inducement, as a matter of course, brought out a very lively competition, and many cases of Artificial Limbs appeared in the Fair, and several exhibitions in walking on Artificial Limbs took place during the Fair, to the no small amusement of the large concourse of people that gathered there upon the anouncement appearing in the papers, that such a novel affair as a *Cripple Race*, was to take place. Every one has probably seen some of the many accounts of it that appeared in the public prints at the time, some of which are here published, relative to the fair as well as the race.

The following is cut from the *New York Times:*

We examined MARKS' Artificial Limbs, and saw some examples of their use that were interesting and satisfactory. These limbs consist of the simplest possible conditions. The ankle is firmly attached, and depends on the elasticity of the india rubber foot, for the required facility in walking. The elegance, naturalness and efficiency of these Artificial Limbs make them almost perfect.

From the *New York Herald*, October 16, 1865:

AMERICAN INSTITUTE FAIR.—The cripple race, which created so much interest on Saturday last, will be repeated to-day. The manufacturers of other Artificial Legs will compete with Mr. Marks for the laurels he gained on that day. Dodworth's full band will be present.

From the *New York Tribune*, October 16, 1865:

AMERICAN INSTITUTE FAIR—PRACTICAL TEST OF ARTIFICIAL LEGS.—The practical test of the merits of Artificial Legs on exhibition at the American Institute Fair, on Saturday evening, was both novel and attractive. It consisted of a walking match along the centre aisle of the Fair building. Three gentlemen entered the list, and gave a specimen of their facility in walking on these substitutes for natural legs. The first contestant, Mr. Bates, was a tall, heavy man, over six feet high. and weighing over 200 pounds. He wore a pair of artificial legs he had used less than three weeks, and therefore walked somewhat unsteadily. The second competitor, Mr. Auzburger, followed, wearing but one artificial leg. He walked a fourth of a mile without a cane in four minutes with apparent ease,·and was warmly applauded. Mr. Frank Stewart closed the performance, wearing two artificial legs, applied just below the knee. He walked a half mile in nine minutes without a cane, with so much spirit, ease and naturalness, that he was frequently obstructed and taken hold of by persons who could not believe that he wore two artificial legs, and he was finally obliged to take the large stand and exhibit the legs and feet to the audience, when he was loudly applauded. All of these gentlemen wore the artificial leg and patent India-rubber foot manufactured by Mr. A. A. Marks, No. 575 Broadway. there were two other gentlemen present, each wearing two of Mr. Marks' legs, having lost their own while in the service of their country.

This walking match originated with Managers Carpenter and Ely, and was superintended by the managers in person, the object being to enable the thousands of legless soldiers to avail themselves of the benefits of a fair trial of the real working merits of the many artificial legs constantly thrust upon their attention.

There are several exhibitors of artificial limbs in the Fair, most if not all of whom are expected to give a sample of the walking capability of their respective limbs at the walking match which takes place this evening at 8 o'clock. A prize will be awarded to the most successful maker.

The *Soldiers' Friend,* of November, after giving a very general account of the races, &c., closes with the following:

Several other exhibitions took place during the fair. The gold medal was awarded to Dr. Marks. The "Rubber Foot," manufactured at this establishment under special patents, has an elasticity and durability that must make the limb welcome to every wearer. The award of the Committee, after a careful examination, is a high testimonial in its favor.

The following official report and decision of the Judges, speaks for itself:

ARTIFICIAL LIMBS.

The Judges on these important Articles were Professor J. M. Carnochan, Professor J. C. V. Smith, and James Knight, M. D., and after a careful and extended examination and practical testing of the various kinds of Limbs on exhibition, awarded the First Premium GOLD MEDAL to Mr. A. A. Marks, for his limbs with India Rubber Hands and Feet.

No. 559, A. A. Marks, 575 Broadway, N. Y. For Artificial Limbs, for simplicity of construction and durability. GOLD MEDAL.

The above cuts are *fac similes* of both sides of the MEDAL, awarded as stated in the above report.

There never was before, in all probability, such a thorough test, impartial and searching investigation in every way, and, too, by so many eminent persons as composed the Judges and Jurors, *too, as it were*, on this very important trial.

FIRST PREMIUM AGAIN.

The American Institute held no Fair in 1866, but in 1867 it again put forth its energies, and held the most successful and brilliant Exhibition, far outdoing its many preceding instructive entertainments, known as the 37th Annual Fair. The contest was again invited. The By-Laws of the Institute had been changed in such a manner as to require the Judges in their investigations to take into consideration ALL THE DIFFERENT ARTICLES OF THEIR CLASS OF WHICH THEY HAD ANY KNOWLEDGE WHETHER ON EXHIBITION OR NOT. The Chairman of the Board of Managers stated PUBLICLY at the close of the Fair that the Board had determined to elevate the standard of excellence in articles on exhibition, by declining to give the FIRST PREMIUM to any Article, unless it was pronounced by competent judges of GREAT utility and equal or SUPERIOR to any like article known to them WHETHER ON EXHIBITION OR NOT. The result on Artificial Limbs is found in the following official report:

No. 238. Marks' Patent Artificial Limbs, have frequently been before the Institute. and continue to sustain their former reputation.

Professor A. K. GARDNER,
" J. C. V. SMITH,
J. J. CRAVEN, M.D., { Judges.

The First Premium was consequently awarded, consisting of the LARGE BRONZE MEDAL (as here shown) and Diploma, thereby indorsing and confirming the action of the eminent Judges at the last Institute Fair, "1865," and at the same time agreeing with the vast numbers who have SOUGHT, FOUND, TRIED and PROVEN by STERN experience, the great superiority of these Artificial Limbs.

1869 FOLLOWS IN SUCCESSION OF 1865 AND 1867.

At this great Exhibition there was increased activity in contending for the *First Premiums* in all branches of goods and wares on exhibition, as exhibitors have learned to value these awards in proportion as the Institute has advanced in popularity and greatness.

The contest in Artificial Limbs was lively and the investigation by the Judges, (*they being required by the By-Laws of the institute to take into consideration all the different articles of their class of which they had any knowledge of WHETHER ON EXHIBITION OR NOT,*) in testing the merits of the Limbs were thorough, searching and convincing, as would be expected from men of their high standing, being well known leading professional and learned men of the present day.

Annexed hereto you will find the report of the Judges, which was inserted upon the *large Diploma* accompanying the Medal of 1869; it tells its own story.

No. 44, ARTIFICIAL LIMBS, A. A. MARKS' BEST.—This Limb is constructed with an India-Rubber Foot, which from its elasticity, does away with the necessity of motion at the ankle joint, and also obviates entirely that *heavy thumping sound* when the foot strikes the ground in walking; an objection which exists in *all other* Artificial Legs which the Committee have any knowledge of. The control which the wearer has over it, and its movements so closely resembling those of the natural limb, as well as the small cost of keeping it in repair (*almost nothing*) entitle it to the highest commendation.

LEWIS A. SAYRE, M. D.,) *Judges.*
JAS. R. McGREGOR, M. D.,)

A true copy from the Report on file.

JOHN W. CHAMBERS, *Secretary*

Upon this very plain, careful and elaborate report, the Board of Managers awarded the FIRST PREMIUM, consisting of *Large Bronze Medal and Diploma.*

1870!—AGAIN PRONOUNCED THE BEST!

1865, 1867 and 1869—Indorsed and Approved in 1870.

Four First Premiums in succession have been awarded by the American Institute for *Marks' Patent Artificial Limbs*, being the only Fairs held by the Institute since 1859. The 39th Fair of the American Institute, held in the autumn of 1870, at the Empire Rink, New York City, was universally admitted to be by far the best managed, best attended, most instructive and brilliant Exhibition ever presented to the people of the United States by this time-honored and world-renowned Institution up to this time. The interest heretofore manifested by exhibitors generally was increased, and the very best Judges were selected.

The following Report of the Judges on Artificial Limbs speaks for itself :

NO. 3. MARKS' ARTIFICIAL LIMBS.

A. A. MARKS. 575 Broadway. New York.

BEST!

The especial point of excellence appears to us to be the *India Rubber Foot*, by the use of which all complications in the construction of an Ankle-joint are avoided.

FRANK H. HAMILTON. M. D.,
HARNEY S. GAY, M. D.,
WM. H. VANBUREN, M. D.,
Judges.

A true copy from the report on file.

JOHN W. CHAMBERS,
Secretary.

Upon this comprehensive report, the Board of Managers Awarded the *First Premium*, consisting of *Large Bronze Medal and Diploma.*

1871.—The By-Laws were changed, and no Medals or Diplomas awarded in any case, the Judges giving a written Report instead, which is embodied in the following extract:

The Artificial Legs with India Rubber Feet, are especially recommended for their *simplicity, durability,* and *easy movement.*

1872.—By-Laws again changed, and Diplomas awarded. *Diploma,* with the following Report inscribed:

The Artificial Limbs manufactured by Mr. Marks continue to merit approval, and are entitled to *all* the confidence the public have to this time reposed in them.

JOHN OSBORN, M. D.,   }
HARVEY S. GAY. M D.,   } *Judges.*
FRANK H. HAMILTON, M. D.,   }

1873.—Artificial Limbs. Report of Judges:

After full and impartial examination of the articles above described, the undersigned Judges make report that they find the Artificial Limbs, on exhibition by A. A. Marks, worthy of the confidence heretofore reposed on them. We cheerfully endorse all that has been said of them by former examinations: *their Simple Construction, Easy Movement, Durability, &c.* First Premium, LARGE SILVER MEDAL.

JOHN OSBORN, M. D.,   }
D. F. FETTER, M. D.,   } *Judges.*
C. D. VARLEY, M. D.,   }

1874.—Report of Judges. Artificial Limbs: A. A. Marks.

We consider the Artificial Limbs of A. A. Marks of great value. *A great improvement—better than any known to us:* and of their grade, entitled to the *highest award.*
A Silver Medal awarded in 1873, as the *Best,* a Diploma of *Maintained Superiority* awarded.

V. P. GIBNEY, M. D.,   }
H. B. SANDS, M. D.,   } *Judges.*
F. G. JANEWAY, M. D.,   }

1875.—A. A. MARKS. Artificial Limbs. No. 13, Dep't 3, Group 5. Judges' Report:

After a full and impartial examination of the articles above described, the undersigned Judges make report that the Artificial Limbs presented by Mr. Marks, are the same as those offered by him at former Exhibitions. We regard them as *Superior to all others* in *Practical Efficiency* and *Simplicity,* and would respectfully recommend the award of a Diploma of *Maintained Superiority.*

FRANCIS A. THOMAS, M. D.,   }
CHARLES W. PACKARD. M. D.,   } *Judges.*
J. R. McGREGOR, M. D.,   }

Further comment is deemed wholly unnecessary.

LETTERS FROM EMINENT SURGEONS.

Among the many eminent surgeons who recommend these Limbs to their patients and those who need Artificial Substitutes, will be found in the following letters, which are published by permission:

NEW YORK. March 20, 1866.

A. A. MARKS, ESQ.:

Sir:—I have examined with great care your patent Artificial Limbs, and cheerfully bear testimony as to the simplicity and efficiency of the invention.

From their peculiar mechanism they perfectly fulfil the purpose for which they were intended, and in my opinion have *no superior* at present in use.

Very respectfully, JOHN J. CRANE, M. D.,
Surgeon to Bellevue Hospital.

795 BROADWAY, NEW YORK, March 21, 1866.

A. A. MARKS, ESQ.:

Dear Sir :—I have had frequent occasion to apply your most valuable Patent Artificial Leg, in cases where I have unfortunately been compelled to mutilate my Patients by amputation, and the admirable imitation which your substitute has given of the original Limb, and the perfect satisfaction to the wearer, is the highest possible commendation that I can give it.

LEWIS A. SAYRE, M. D.
Professor of Surgery, Bellevue Hospital, Medical College.

Office of ROBERT S. NEWTON, M. D.,
22 East 18th Street, between Broadway and Fifth Ave.
NEW YORK, March 22, 1866.

A. A. MARKS, ESQ., 575 Broadway, N. Y.:

Dear Sir :—Having been well acquainted with your Artificial Limbs and various improvements which you have made for the last ten years, and from the great success which has attended the application of your limbs, and the utility of the same, I have no hesitation in saying that their accomplishments have not been surpassed.

The ease and facility with which persons move and walk about, and run as it were, is such, that in many cases the Artificial Limb cannot be detected.

Yours truly, ROBERT S. NEWTON, M. D.

No. 80 Irving Place, NEW YORK, May 24, 1866.

A. A. MARKS, ESQ.:

Dear Sir :—I have carefully examined your Artificial Limbs, and believe, because of their simplicity and strength, that they will be sought for by those who may be so unfortunate as to require them.

Very Truly Yours, &c.,
JAMES R. WOOD, M. D.,
Surgeon to Bellevue Hospital, Professor of Operative and Surgical Pathology, Bellevue Hospital, Medical College. &c., &c.

COCHECTON, SULLIVAN COUNTY.
NEW YORK, March 14, 1865.

MR. A. A. MARKS :

Dear Sir :—I have worn your Patent Leg for the last year. I am well pleased with it. It has not required the least repairs. I can walk better with it than any leg I ever used, *except the natural one.*

I consider your India Rubber Foot a valuable improvement to Artificial Legs.

Respectfully yours,
W. L. APPLEY, M. D.

FLEMINGTON, NEW JERSEY.
March 1, 1876.

MR. A. A. MARKS:

Dear Sir:—It is now more than two years since you fitted my son with one of your Artificial Legs, and sufficient time has elapsed to form an opinion as to its merits.

I think your claim for "superiority of your Artificial Limbs over all others, in practical efficiency, simplicity of construction and durability", is well founded, and cannot honestly be denied. I will also add that for ease and comfort in use they cannot be surpassed.

Yours truly,

W. H. SCHENK. M. D.

ELIZABETHPORT, NEW JERSEY.
March 31, 1876.

MR. A. A. MARKS:

Dear Sir:—Having for the last eleven years used in my practice your Patent Artificial Limbs, with India Rubber attachments, I feel it my privilege as well as duty to acknowledge my favorable appreciation of them.

Several of the cases have been under my daily observation while in pursuance of their various avocations, the majority being employees of the Central Railroad of New Jersey, of which I have been a long time connected as surgeon. I will only mention a single case, that of Patrick Libby, of this place, whom you supplied with a pair of Limbs for the lower extremities, sixteen months ago. Fortunately both knee joints had been preserved, and he has since the application been able to perform considerable amount of walking, and usually without any cane, regarding it as an encumbrance. I met him yesterday, and although he does not fully conceal his infirmity, his movements are easy and do not call up the unpleasent sympathy which observers so often have to feel for the unfortunate.

I may, if desired by consent of the parties, refer to others having lost one lower extremity, who almost or wholly succeed in their natural desire to escape observation ; another remark is due, that the India Rubber foot does *not* produce that WOODEN LEG SOUND, so often noticed on the street from *less* modern appliances. I have not yet heard a patient express dissatisfaction, and feel well sustained by experience in giving this approval.

Yours truly,

J. S. MARTIN. M. D.,
Late Surgeon 14th Reg. New Jersey Vol.

WASHINGTON, NORTH CAROLINA.
February 12th 1876.

MR. A. A. MARKS :

Dear Sir :—Having been so unfortunate as to lose my right leg, four inches below the knee, by having the bone crushed in a wheel of my Buggy, which necessitated amputation, I feel it my duty to offer you such testimony, as I feel guaranteed in giving, after four years' use of one of your Patent Artificial Legs. Like most persons who have thus been disabled, I felt that all prospects of success in a business, point of view, had been destroyed by the loss of my limb ; but I earnestly declare that with one of your Artificial Limbs, I can get about and attend to my professional duties, (*Physician in active practice*) just about as well as before the accident occured to me.

Before purchasing, I visited several cities and took pains to examine all the inventions I could find of this kind, and can confidently assert that yours is by far more *secure*, *simple* and *durable* than any I could find ; I can walk astonishingly well, in fact, so naturally, that some of the ignorant people in my section actually believe that my leg has grown out again.

Very truly and gratefully yours,

JOHN McDONALD, M. D.

No. 146 Fourth Street, Brooklyn. E. D., New York, May 16th, 1876.

MR. A. A. MARKS—*Dear Sir:* I have thoroughly examined the case of the boy, THOMAS KEHR, of this city, who has been wearing a pair of your Artificial Legs for the past six months. About a year and a half ago, he was run over by a train of the S. S. R. R. of Long Island and both of his lower limbs were so crushed that I amputated them, the one well above the knee, the other about one inch and a half below. At the time of the operation many expressed a wish that death would occur, as the lad being very poor it was thought that his future would not only be a burden to himself but that his future support, should he reach man's estate, would depend upon the charity of the public, as it was considered about an impossibility for him to serviceably use Artificial Limbs. I am thankful that I can say that you have made his future worth the living, by giving him the means of good locomotion. I saw him two weeks after he had put them on for the first time, and it astonished me greatly to see the remarkable use he had already acquired; since then I have seen him *many* times, and have each time seen marked improvement in the freedom of use in walking. Within the past week I saw him walking on the street, without even the help of a cane, and so little lamed that any person seeing him, would not for a moment have the least suspicion that he was using legs other than such as nature provided; there is only the slightest limp in the right leg.

I feel competent to say, that in this case your Artificial Limbs have proved a *grand success.* I have never before seen Artificial Limbs, which in action, approached so near that of perfection. I attribute the wonderful success in this boy's case, mainly to the superior results achieved by your inventions. Especially can attention be called to the use of the Rubber Foot, thereby dispensing with the ankle joint, thus giving the wearer an ELASTIC, RELIABLE and SURE FOOTING, which must greatly relieve him from the care and WATCHFULNESS which must certainly be required by those who wear Artificial Limbs having jointed feet. Your plain and simple mode of construction of Artificial Legs is to my mind *unquestionably* the BEST, and when asked by poor legless persons, as to whose make of Artificial Limbs would prove the best to secure for comfort and utility, I most decidedly say without any hesitation, MARKS'!

Very Respectfully,

SAMUEL J. BRADY, M. D.

[For Illustration of this case see page 26.]

The following letters are from persons who have been wearing MARKS' Patent Artificial Legs for several of the past years, and speak for themselves:

** These stars indicate that the Artificial Limbs, in each of these cases were fitted from measure and sent to the persons without their coming to the manufactory to be fitted. Full information on this subject will be found in the after part of this pamphlet.

[AMPUTATION ABOVE KNEE.]

EASTON, PA., July 31, 1866.

MR. A. A. MARKS:

Dear Sir:—It gives me sincere pleasure to be able to inform you that the Artificial Limb which you made for me has more than realized your promises and my own expectations. You are aware that previous to procuring your Patent Limb, I had worn one of Dr.———make about six months. I can assert the supremacy of your limb over his in no stronger way than by stating the fact that since I have procured yours, I have not worn that made by Dr.———a single day.

Your limb gives a more elastic, springy, life-like motion to my step, removes the clattering noise incident to the use of the ankle joint. and fits the stump much more comfortable, the knee joint too works STILL and admirably, and just as good as new, yet I have given it some severe trials. I have walked seven miles in one day, which I think is pretty good for a leg above the knee.

After having examined most of the Artificial Limbs in this country. I pronounce unhesitatingly in favor of yours, both for durability, usefullness, comfort and appearance.—Yours respectfully.

NOTE.—This gentleman prefers to not have his name appear here, but the publisher is at liberty to give it to any individual who wishes it.—This gentleman (*near ten years later*) continues to wear the same limb.

[LEG ABOVE KNEE.]

NEW YORK, February 13th, 1871.

MR. A. A. MARKS,

Dear Sir:—It gives me great pleasure to state that after having used one of your Patent Artificial Legs for over six months, I find it to be superior to the legs of other makers that I have used before. It is safer to stand or walk on, does not produce the creaking and rattling noise which greatly annoyed me in the others, is easily kept clean and in good working order.

I can walk a longer distance with less exertion and fatigue than with the other, and can stand with my whole weight on it without fear of it bending under me. I do cheerfully recommend your Patent Artificial Leg, as superior to any that I have worn.

Very respectfully,

FREDERICK GUYER,

Late Cap. Co. "D." 83d N. Y. V. (9th N. S. M.)

NOTE—Capt. Guyer, is still using same limb (1876).

[LEG ABOVE KNEE.]

POST-OFFICE, OXFORD, NEW HAVEN CO., CONN.,

February 9th, 1876.

A. A. MARKS, ESQ.,

Dear Sir:—At the Battle of Cedar Creek, October 19th, 1864, I gave to Uncle Sam my right leg, above the knee, and in 1865 received in exchange one of the ——— manufacture, "which I considered at the time a very good substitute for the BUTLER Leg:" but the continual repairing which it required, caused me to seek one of a more simple construction.

In 1870, "as you are well aware," I received one of your manufacture, which I have since worn with satisfaction, so much so that when I am in need of another I shall give you a call.

Yours, very respectfully,

C. H. BUTLER, Postmaster.

[LEG ABOVE KNEE.]

LAW OFFICE OF GEORGE W. PINCKNEY,
185 Montague Street, opposite Academy of Music,
BROOKLYN, NEW YORK, February 25th, 1876.

MR. A. A. MARKS,

Dear Sir:—I respectfully state that I am now using and have used for the last seven years, your Patent Artificial Leg, with Rubber Foot without ankle-joint.

The first leg I had was——————————which had the ankle-joint, wooden foot, &c., which gave me much trouble in its not being reliable, and repeatedly needing repairs. You applied a Rubber Foot, and next the knee-joint gave out, and I was compelled to give it up. I then purchased a new leg of your make, and used it continually ever since without a cent's repairs. I cheerfully recommend your Leg.

Yours, respectfully,

GEO. W. PINCKNEY,

[LEG ABOVE KNEE.]

WATERTOWN, March 27th, 1876,

MR. A. A. MARKS:

Dear Sir:—I, having used Artificial Legs for the last twenty-four years, with ankle-joints, both tenon and ball and socket. Two years since I was prevailed upon to get you to repair my leg, by putting on your Rubber Foot, without ankle-joint. I certainly was prejudiced against the stiff ankle at first, but after using it for a while I became so strong a convert that I ordered a new leg (as you are aware) and sent my measures accordingly, to be fitted without my presence. The leg came in due time, and fits to a charm, and works to perfection in every way. When asked whose leg I wear, I tell them that I wear one of your Artificial Legs, and have *only 2½ inches of stump* from the body. They express wonder and astonishment that I can get around so well, and often say no one would think that I had a *wooden leg.*

I certainly can recommend your limb highly, having worn other kinds so long, I claim to be capable of judging of their merits.

Hoping you may live long to benefit others as you have me.

I remain, yours, very truly,

F. A. WEBB.

[LEG ABOVE KNEE.]

CHATHAM VILLAGE, COLUMBIA CO., NEW YORK.

MR. A. A. MARKS,

Dear Sir:—It gives me great satisfaction to state that your Patent Artificial Leg, with Rubber Foot, has given me the greatest satisfaction.

After wearing one of Dr. —— for five years. I think I ought to be a judge of the merits of Artificial Legs. The one of Dr. —— was continually out of order—the cords were breaking every day or two—then I had to take the crutches until I could send and get it repaired : and then, the tormenting clatter it most always had, made me ashamed to go in company, and the expense in keeping in repairs, (over sixty dollars), besides the inconvenience. I had but little faith, at first sight, of your leg, without an ankle-joint, but was willing to do most anything to get rid of the trouble I had before, and get something that I could rely on, but was happily disappointed. I have worn the leg you made for me for over five years: there has not been a day in that time that it has not served me well. The Rubber Foot is the best improvement yet. I want no more ankle-joints in Artificial Legs to bother me. Take it altogether, I think it is the most perfect leg I have seen. Now, let me tell you what I do with it : I am a builder, and I have to go upon scaffolds and roofs, and even on church steeples, too. I take my share in any work as it comes, and have shingled the spire of a church when none of the men in my employ would do it on account of the wind. I have walked two miles in the morning and done a day's work : in fact, I do almost everything that I ever did before I lost my leg. My experience teaches me that yours is superior to *all others,*

Yours respectfully,

JAMES G. ALLEN.

[LEG ABOVE KNEE.]

BLACKSTOCK, CHESTER CO., SOUTH CAROLINA.

February 23d, 1876.

MR. A. A. MARKS, 575 Broadway, N. Y. City :

Dear Sir :—I have been wearing your Patent Artificial Leg for over a year, and consider it the best Artificial Leg I ever used ; there is no clanking sound as I walk, like others which I have used, the clanking of which was very disagreeable. The Rubber foot is a success; it manœuvres admirably; moves as soft and nicely as the natural foot. I have only 5½ inch stump from hip joint, therefore I labor under more disadvantage than most of my maimed brothers, I freely recommend your leg to all maimed soldiers, as the best in use.

JOHN CARROLL.

[LEG ABOVE KNEE.]

GREENBUSH, WISCONSIN,
February 28th 1876.

A. A. MARKS:

Dear Sir :—I wish to give my testimony in recommending your Patent Artificial Leg, with rubber foot. I have worn the one I had of you over four years, and never paid out one cent for repairs. I have seen and worn other kinds of limbs ; they have too much machinery about them for a common mechanic to understand and keep in repairs. I cheerfully recommend yours in preference to ALL others that have come under my observation.

Yours truly,
CHAS. A. CORBETT.

[LEG ABOVE KNEE.]

PITTSBURG, IOWA,
February 15th 1876.

Mr. MARKS :

Dear Sir :—I have used your leg long enough to satisfy me that they are far ahead of any others, for ease to the wearer and durability. My experience with others, and over four years in wearing this, satisfy me of their superiority.

FRANKLIN W. REED.

[LEG ABOVE KNEE.]

HOLYOKE MASS., February 21st, 1876.

Mr. A. A. MARKS :

Dear Sir :—I am glad to give my testimony in regard to your Artificial Leg, which I have worn for the last five years, and can say of its merits, to be one of the best legs that the government provides for its soldiers, who lost their legs in the late war. My first leg was made by——,I wore it for five years, and could never feel safe to leave home on it, for it was sure to give out, and the rattle trap in the ankle could be heard across the street. I finally concluded to take one of your legs with rubber foot, and am proud to say was never sorry. I feel safe now to leave home, and work all day at circular saw bench, as well as a man with two sound legs. Your leg is good for the poor, as well as the rich ; I think nobody will ever go back on your leg after trying it.

Yours faithfully,
SAMUEL S. CHAPMAN.

[LEG ABOVE KNEE.]

Office of A. A. HALL,
Dealer in Fine Jewelry, Watches and Silverware,
EAST RANDOLPH, NEW YORK, February 15th, 1876.

MR. A. A. MARKS :

Dear Sir : When I was discharged from the U. S. Army, I was furnished with an Artificial Leg, with heel cords and ankle joint, which I wore for five years and it was continually getting out of repair, which annoyed me very much ; and now, after wearing one of your limbs with Rubber Foot, for over five years (except one sett of suspenders) and the limb is apparently as good now as when new. I cheerfully recommend them to all requiring Artificial substitutes as the best, as it is the safest and most natural of any there is made so far as my knowledge extends,

Yours respectfully,
A. A. HALL,
Late Company E. 9th N. Y. Cav.

** [LEG ABOVE KNEE.]

WHEATON, DUPAGE CO., ILL.

MR. A. A. MARKS:

Dear Sir :—I have worn one of your make of Artificial Legs for nearly five years, and am exceedingly well pleased with it ; in that time it has not cost me one dollar for repairs ; that is quite well considering that I weigh 230 lbs.

The Rubber Foot is a grand invention ; no squeaking, no getting out of order ; it can be depended upon, and the knee joint too is the best and strongest I ever saw. I had another manufacturer of Artificial Limbs tell me it was the strongest and best knee joint made, and I think my weight and work has proved it. The limb I had before yours, broke right down with my weight. In my opinion your limbs are the best as well as cheapest,

Yours respectfully,

H. E. AUSTIN.

[LEG ABOVE KNEE.]

KEELER, VAN BUREN CO., MICH.,
February 13th, 1876.

MR. A. A. MARKS:

Dear Sir :—I have worn one of your Patent Artificial Legs now for nearly five years, and it bids fair to last me another five to come ; it has needed but very little repairs. I have worn one of———and it cost me fifty dollars more than the one you made me, besides innumerable repairs, for it was continually getting out of order, besides the rattle and clatter it made was enough to drive one wearing them insane with vexation, and which is obviated by your Rubber Foot. I cheerfully recommend your limbs.

Yours truly,

JOHN TAYLOR.

[LEG ABOVE KNEE.]

LOCKRIDGE, JEFFERSON CO., IOWA,
February 12th, 1876.

MR. A. A. MARKS :

Dear Sir :—It is now five years since I received a government order for an Artificial Leg, which I chose to have you make for me, and which I have worn ever since, doing a veriety of work. Part of the time I have worked at my trade (house carpenter and painter) going up and down ladders and working on staging ; in fact doing all kinds of work, so that the durability of your patent has, I think, been fully tested, as the foot appears to be as good now as when I first commenced to wear it, over five years ago

I have a small piece of land which I cultivate in fruit, both large and small. Last fall I cut and carried to the fruit house, 2500 lbs. of grapes ; so you may know I did some walking on my Artificial Leg. It has given me perfect satisfaction. I like the Rubber Foot without ankle joint, on account of its durability and it making no clattering noise.

Yours respectfully,

ROBERT STEVENSON.

[LEG ABOVE KNEE.]

WINNEBAGO CITY, MINN.,
January 10th, 1876.

Mr. A. A. Marks :

Dear Sir :—I have worn the leg you made for over five years, and it is good for quite a spell yet. It is the best that I have used or examined ; very simple in construction and very durable, by its having a Rubber Foot, making it easy to walk on, my leg being off above knee, and with this I can do almost all kinds of work with ease,

Yours &c.,

JEROME B. FRAZEE.

[LEG ABOVE KNEE.]

BUENA VISTA, MARION CO., GEORGIA,
February 31st, 1876.

Mr. A. A. MARKS:

Dear Sir:—Your Artificial Leg is the best I ever saw. I have used other kinds, and know well of what I am speaking. The five years service I have had with this of your make, and your efforts to meet the wants of your customers on reasonable terms, induce me to recommend your limbs to ALL needing them.

Yours, &c.,

JAMES M. LOWE.

[LEG ABOVE KNEE AND ARM ABOVE ELBOW.]

BINGHAMTON, NEW YORK,
April 9th, 1876.

Mr. A. A. MARKS:

Dear Sir:—I learn that you are going to print a new Pamphlet, if so I would like very well to tell my story:—In October, 1867, I was accidently caught on a large circular saw, 4 feet in diameter, and my Right Arm and Right Leg were so fearfully mutilated that both had to be amputated above the elbow and knee. In March, '68, after looking around very thoroughly I purchased my Artificials of you, and am now compelled to say that after eight years of constant use I feel confident that I made no mistake in taking your Patent. The repairs have been comparatively small; and are in very good condition now. I often walk to church, over a mile, in company with others, and have no difficulty in keeping up with them, and although my walk is slightly defective, many persons whom I frequently meet have no idea of my being so *largely* Artificial,

I am rather over medium size and weight, and having a stump but eight inches from the body, feel well satisfied with my getting about. The Arm is not of very much service, the stump being less than 8 inches long, but I would not be without it for the price of two or three; it certainly has exceeded your representation in regard to utility. I go all over my farm, climb fences, and see to all the work, and do considerable myself, get in and out of my waggon very comfortably and transact all my business. When walking about I generally use a cane, but often forget it and go about for hours without any, and get around much better than any one would suppose under the circumstances.

Yours, &c.,

B. W. LAWRENCE.

The following few letters are from persons using the Knee Bearing Legs.

[LEG. KNEE BEARING.]

EDWARD MANCHER, OPTICIAN,
55 South Clark Street, opposite Sherman House,
CHICAGO, ILL., February 11th, 1876.

MR. A. A. MARKS, New York City:

Dear Sir:—It affords me great satisfaction to report to you that the first leg received from you, (over five years ago), has far exceeded my expectations, in durability and general usefulness, which is principally owing to the simplicity of the leg. My second leg made by you last Summer, proves still better, and I could not possibly be tempted to try again any other manufacturer's article, because I walk so well that a great many of my friends and acquaintances, do not know that I walk with a false leg. I never hesitate to recommend your legs to all whom I meet, who are compelled by misfortune to use an Artificial Leg.

I am, yours most respectfully,

EDWARD MANCHER.

[LEG, KNEE BEARING.]

CAZENOVIA, NEW YORK,
February 23d, 1876.

A. A. MARKS:

Dear Sir :—With honest pleasure do I respond to your invitation to say a word about my experience with the Artificial Limb of your manufacture.
For several years I wore one of ——— make, but it was far from satisfactory, on account of the rattle and the clapping of the foot ; I then tried yours, and ever since have walked with *less irritation, more easily,* and with scarcely any ATTRACTABLE NOISE. It is so simple in construction that it does not get out of order. I have now worn mine nearly *five years*, and it has cost me less than *one dollar* for repairs. I can unhesitatingly say that your Limb is the best with which I have yet become acquainted.
Very truly yours,
ISAAC N. CLEMENTS.

[LEG, KNEE BEARING.]

VINELAND, CUMBERLAND CO., NEW JERSEY,
June 2d, 1875.

MR. A. A. MARKS :

Dear Sir :—I desire to take a new Govt. Leg from you, as I am more than satisfied with your make. I have worn the Govt. Leg you made me in 1870, every day since, now *almost* five years, and KNOW the merits of it so well that I don't intend to wear any other make after the trials I had with them heretofore.
Yours, respectfully,
.WILLIAM D. SMITH.

[LEG, KNEE BEARING.]

PATTERSON NEW JERSEY, 111 Willis Street,
February 15th, 1876.

MR. A. A. MARKS :

Dear Sir :—My several years of hard work on your Patent Leg, after the trials I have experienced on other kinds compel me to say in all candor and truth that your's is far the best in *all* respects.
Yours, &c.,
JAMES RAWSON.

From the list of cases of double amputations of legs which have been treated by me, you will find in the following letters what *they* have to say about them. Mr. January's case, which is represented by the engravings, is worthy of special notice, yet many of them do as well as Mr. J.

Fig. 14 is engraved from a photograph taken of Mr. John W. January, of Minonk, Illinois, late Corporal Co. B, 14th Regt. Illinois Cavalry, who lost both his legs in the war, and to whom I applied a pair of Artificial Legs in 1865, on government orders. He was then a mere skeleton, just from the hospital, and weighing but sixty pounds. Now, in January, 1876, after taking a new pair of Government Legs, he sits for his picture, and his present condition, with Artificial Legs removed (yet in position to be seen), and also his bare stumps are clearly shown.

Fig. 15.

Fig. 14.

Fig. 15 was taken at same time and speaks for itself also; he is now in order for business; good health, present weight, 180 pounds. Few men of sound, natural limbs perform more actual labor than Mr. January does, he owning and working a large farm, engaged in other active business pursuits, and also holding the important and responsible position of Town Collector. This illustrates a single case of both amputations of Legs below the knees, showing that persons are by no means helpless who have been thus disabled. Over fifty additional cases of double amputations have been furnished with my patent Artificial Limbs, with gratifying success.

(Mr. January will cheerfully answer any letters addressed to him upon the subject.)

[BOTH LEGS AMPUTATED BELOW KNEES.]

NEW BOSTON, NEW HAMPSHIRE, May 10, 1866.
MR. A. A. MARKS:

Dear Sir :—Nearly a year has passed since you fixed me up upon my legs again, and it occurs to me that, my case being rather an extraordinary one, you would like to give it to the public through your pamphlet.

When I decided to take your legs from the government, I had examined all the various kinds that the government had adopted, and concluded to take yours for the reasons which I will give.

Having been in the hospital for some time, I had seen many soldiers who had been provided with Artificial Limbs, and witnessed the many troubles and annoyances as well as expenses to which they were constantly subjected in most kinds of limbs, and saw that your patents were clear from all these tormenting trials, and at the same time discovered that your patients walked with more ease, comfort and natural step than the other kinds with their clattering ankle-joints. My experience has only added to the high opinion I formerly had gathered of your limbs.

My weight is over 200 pounds, and although both legs are now Artificial, I can do almost everything that I formerly could—can take a pail of water in each hand and walk off readily, and do work generally required about the farm.

I earnestly advise all my unfortunate friends to purchase your plain, substantial, and *always* reliable Patent Limbs.
Yours very truly,
CALVIN BATES,
Late Corp'l 20th Reg't Maine Vols.

NOTE.—Mr. Bates continues to reside at same place, and also continues to wear same kind of Artificial Limbs.

BOTH LEGS AMPUTATED—ONE ABOVE, THE OTHER BUT ONE INCH BELOW THE KNEE.]

KINGSTON, ONTARIO, CANADA,
February, 1876.
A. A. MARKS, ESQ., N. Y. City :

Dear Sir :—In regard to my Artificial Legs, I can inform you that I am *more* than pleased with them. When I lost both my legs Railroading, I felt that I didn't care to live, when I thought of the helpless life I supposed was before me ; but thanks for your valuable inventions, by which I am enabled to once more walk on *terra firma.* I have used them for six years, and no repairs needed, yet I do a great deal of walking and use but one cane.
Yours truly,
MATTHEW GORMAN.

[BOTH LEGS AMPUTATED BELOW KNEES.]

PROVIDENCE, R. I., November 10th, 1875.
A. A. MARKS, 575 Broadway, N. Y. City :

Dear Sir :—Having worn a *pair* of your patent Artificial Legs for over five years, and had an abundance of experience of other kinds prior to using yours, have no hesitation whatever in pronouncing yours by far the best in every essential point. I do a variety of labor on my *pair* of legs with ease and comfort, and take much pains to recommend your patent limbs to all I see needing Artificial ones.
Yours respectfully,
H. F. HICKS.

** [BOTH LEGS AMPUTATED BELOW KNEES.]

CLEVELAND, OHIO, January 27th, 1876.
MR. A. A. MARKS:

Dear Sir :—Having used a pair of Artificial Limbs of your manufacture for a period of five years, I am happy to testify that they are the best limbs that have come to my notice. I am able to walk comfortably without the aid of a cane. My experience in the use of limbs of different manufacture, enables me to judge of their superior qualities and efficiency. I defy any one wearing two of any other kind to walk as well as I do.

Yours respectfully,
WILLIAM MOLHERIN.

[BOTH LEGS AMPUTATED BELOW KNEES.]

MONTREAL, CANADA, February 10th, 1876.

MR. MARKS :

Dear Sir :—It is now over five years since I lost both my legs below the knees, and was supplied by you with a pair of Artificial Limbs. During all this time they have done good service, and proved most satisfactory, never having required any repairs. They are comfortable and easy to walk with, and I get along so *naturally* that some old friends are much surprised when told that they are New Yorkers.

Should this catch the eye of any who have been unfortunate enough to lose a limb, I would confidently recommend them to you.

I remain, dear sir,
Yours respectfully,
JAMES NICKLES.

[BOTH LEGS AMPUTATED BELOW KNEES.]

LINCOLN UNIVERSITY, CHESTER COUNTY, PA.,
February 22d, 1876.

This is to certify that I have had constantly in use two of Mr. A. A. Marks' patent Artificial Limbs since 1871, which I am glad to state have come up to my greatest expectations, on account of their simplicity of construction, being without the complication of bolts, screws, &c., at the ankles ; they have given me very little trouble. The ease, elasticity, comfort, stillness and naturalness occasioned by your Rubber Feet seem to operate truly wonderful.

I earnestly recommend them to all needing Artificial Substitutes.

HAMILTON H. HUGHES.

** [BOTH LEGS AMPUTATED BELOW KNEES.]

LACON, MARSHAL CO., ILLINOIS,
February 28th, 1876.

MR. A. A. MARKS:

Dear Sir :—The Artificial Legs I obtained from you for my son last July have given entire satisfaction, and I believe them to be the best Artificial Legs that are manufactured, and that they give the best of satisfaction to the patient who uses them, as there is no rattling or unnatural noise about them.

I most cheerfully recommend them to all in need of Artificial Limbs.

Yours respectfully,
A. R. CATLIN.

[BOTH LEGS AMPUTATED BELOW KNEES.]

DEPARTMENT OF PUBLIC WORKS,
OTTAWA, CANADA,
February 12th, 1876.

I had the misfortune while I was in Manitoba, in 1871, to have both of my feet so badly frozen that I was obliged to have them amputated above the ankles in 1872. After they had healed I ordered a pair of Artificial Legs from Mr. A. A. Marks' Establishment in New York, and have used them ever since. They give me the greatest satisfaction, and I consider them the best invention of the kind.

I make use of a cane when walking, but might as well dispense with it. My gait is surprisingly natural. A gentleman whom I had been acquainted with for six months, and whom I met almost daily during that time, expressed his astonishment to learn after those six months that I wore Artificial Legs, without his ever having noticed it.

I take much pleasure in recommending Mr. Marks' Establishment to all needing Artificial Limbs.

J. A. THERIAULT.

[BOTH LEGS AMPUTATED BELOW KNEES.]

ELIZABETH, NEW JERSEY, January 25th, 1876.

Mr. A. A. MARKS :

Dear Sir :—My nearly two years experience in wearing a *pair* of your Artificial Legs with Rubber Feet has proved perfectly satisfactory in all respects. I get along so much better than I ever expected to, and my friends, too, are all so well pleased with my walking, that I feel assured, from my own knowledge and what others who are using your limbs say, that there can be no better Artificials than yours.

PATRICK LIBBY.

The following letters are from persons who have suffered single amputations of legs below knees :

[LEG BELOW KNEE.]

GREENVILLE, MERCER CO., PA. February, 1876.

Mr. A. A. MARKS :

Dear Sir :—Allow me to say, for the benefit of those needing Artificial Limbs, that I have worn Artificial Limbs of two different (and once considered) prominent manufacturers, and all the time that I wore them I had nothing but vexation—cords breaking and ankle-joints getting out of repair. In 1870 I procured one of your Patent Legs with Rubber Foot, and with trifling repairs have worn it ever since, with ease and comfort. I walk so well that few ever detect it. My occupation is a tinsmith, and I can climb a ladder and get over a roof of a house as good as any one. I have walked seven miles on railroad track in one hour and three-quarters, on your limb. I consider it the best made at the present time, and would not have any other, especially one with an ankle-joint. The elasticity of the Rubber Foot gives all the motion required.

Hoping that you may live to a good old age, to supply the needy and enjoy the fruits of your labor, is the wish of

Yours truly,
EBENEZER F. BENNETT.
Late Co. B, 76th Regt. Pa. Vols.

**[LEG BELOW KNEE.]

CEDAR FALLS RECORDER, CEDAR FALLS, IOWA. February 11th, 1876.

Mr. A. A. MARKS :

Dear Sir :—It affords me great pleasure to inform you that the Artificial Leg with Rubber Foot, purchased from you and worn constantly by me for the past three years, continues to give entire satisfaction.

I have worn out two other styles of Artificial Legs, and unhesitatingly say that your leg is in all respects far superior to any that have ever come under my observation ; the absence of ankle-joints, cords, springs, and all the other machinery, is, to my mind, an advantage, the importance of which can only be fully appreciated by those who have worn the old style, rattling and squeaking like an infirm threshing machine.

I do not hesitate to say your Leg with Rubber Foot is more durable and economical, inasmuch as there is no complicated machinery to get out of order, easier to use, more pleasant in *every* particular, and especially is this, with your rubber foot the wearer walks erect, and not as is the case with all the other Artificial Legs, with the eyes bent down to the ground. If your leg possessed no other superiority than this alone, it would be far in advance of any that I have ever seen.

You are perfectly at liberty to refer any to me for such information as I have.

Yours, very respectfully,
S. H. PACKARD.

[LEG BELOW KNEE.]

BRIDGEPORT, CONN.,
February 9th 1876.

MR. A. A. MARKS:

Dear Sir—I would respectfully state that I have used your Patent Artificial Leg with India Rubber Foot, for the last three and a half years. Previous to that time I had used the ——, also the ——, and in my opinion the leg manufactured by you, is *far superior* to any others I have seen, for the reason that they are free from the complication of cords, bolts, &c., at the feet, which are used in the others.

I think there are very few who use an Artificial Leg as much as I do; I often hear my friends who have been well acquainted with me for months, express great surprise to learn that I am wearing an Artificial Leg.

I cheerfully recommend all who inquire about Artificial Limbs, to you as the place to get the best.

Respectfully,
A. E. BARTRAM.

[LEG BELOW KNEE.]

LA HARPE, HANCOCK Co., ILL.
February 15th, 1876.

MR. A. A. MARKS:

Dear Sir :—I avail myself of this opportunity to write you a few lines.

I had tried two other kinds before getting yours, and I find that yours is far superior to either of them, both in ease and durability.

The Rubber Foot does away with cords and springs that others have, and are always getting out of order. I cheerfully recommend yours as the best, to all I meet needing Artificial Limbs. I have used yours now five years, and it is in good order yet; it has never cost over two dollars for repairs. I am a large, heavy man, weighing from 230 to 240 lbs., and am going all the time, therefore am very hard on an Artificial Leg. The other two did not last me seven years, they were better than none, but nothing to compare with yours ; I have made application for a new govt. leg of your make, and shall come for it some time this coming Summer.

Yours truly,
WILLIAM BUNGER.
Co. G, 118th Regt. Illinois Infantry.

[LEG BELOW KNEE.]

EDDYVILLE, WAPPELLO Co., IOWA.
February 13th 1876.

MR. A. A. MARKS:

Dear Sir :—Having worn one of your Patent Artificial Legs for five years, and now made application for a new one from the government, of the same kind, seems evident that I am satisfied.

I have worn several other kinds, and recommend yours above *all* others.

Respectfully,
JAMES M. WELSH,
Co. B, 9th Iowa Vols.

[LEG BELOW KNEE.]

WILLIAMSTOWN, MASS., February 16th, 1876

A. A. MARKS :

Dear Sir :—I have worn one of your Artificial Legs for almost five years, and it has given me *perfect* satisfaction ; I wore one of——before yours, and I find yours far superior. The Rubber Foot is a great improvement, as it gives an elastic step, I can walk twice as far and twice as easy as with the other kind. I *always* recommend yours as the *best.*

Yours respctfully,
WILLIAM M. FIELD.

[LEG BELOW KNEE.]

NEW YORK CITY, 50 Pike Street,
February 12th, 1876.

Mr. MARKS :

Dear Sir :—As you are to publish a new pamphlet, I wish to add my name to your long list of patients, who use your Patent Limbs. After using one of yours for several years, I was induced to purchase one with ankle-joint and wooden foot, of Dr.——. It was by no means satisfactory, and after a thorough trial I laid it aside, and am now using yours with entire satisfaction,

Give me the plain, reliable elastic Rubber Foot for all else.

Yours very truly,
MRS. MARIA SISSON.

** [LEG BELOW KNEE.]

PAINESVILLE, LAKE CO., OHIO,
March 31st, 1876.

MR. MARKS :

Dear Sir :—I have been wearing your patent Artificial Leg for over seven years, and it gives me much pleasure to record my testimony in favor of its very important features—its firm, noiseles, light, elastic step in walking. I think it has no equal. I could not be induced to exchange for any other.

Yours truly,
MRS. E. R. GAGE.

[LEG BELOW KNEE.]

SHERIFF'S OFFICE, PLATTE CO., NEBRASKA.
COLUMBUS, February 20th, 1876.

MR. A. A. MARKS :

Dear Sir :—I wish to say, through your pamphlet, a few words to those unlucky ones like myself, especially those who are in need of an Artificial Substitute, and not yet obtained one.

Just consider it in the same light as any other article of necessity in the line of mechanical construction. Mr. Marks' Patent Leg with Rubber Foot is plain, simple and reliable. I have worn it the last five years, and it has proved every way perfectly satisfactory, and have applied for a new Government Leg of his make. I have worn other kinds with the rattling ankle-joints, and want no more of them.

Marks' Leg is the best, and no mistake.

Yours, &c.,
BENJAMIN SPEILMAN,
Sheriff.

Late Co. K, Ohio Vols.

[LEG BELOW KNEE.]

BOILING SPRINGS, PA.,
February 17th, 1876.

MR. A. A. MARKS:

Dear Sir:—I have been using one of your Artificial Legs for five years now, and I think it will last me for some time yet to come.

I have used three different makes, but I prefer yours before any other. The other kinds are always getting out of repair after wearing a couple of months, but Marks' Patent Leg does not need much repairs, except once I broke one of the joints in lifting heavy stones that weighed from two to four hundred pounds each ; I got it repaired, and now it is as good as ever. I am coming out to you to get another some time.

Yours truly,
JAMES A. FELLERS,
Co. I, 87th Pa. Vols.

[LEG BELOW KNEE.]

SALEM, MASS., February 8th, 1876.

MR. MARKS:

Dear Sir:—I most cheerfully add my testimony to the great worth of the Patent Artificial Limbs of your invention and make. I have no hesitation in saying that it is the best limb I have ever used (*except only the one I had previous to the war*). I have used several different kinds, and find yours superior in every respect.

Yours, &c.,
WM. H. GOLDSMITH.

**[LEG BELOW KNEE.]

GILMER, UPSHER CO., TEXAS.
February 15th, 1876.

MR. A. A. MARKS:

Dear Sir:—I have been using one of your Patent Legs since 1871 ; it has never given me any trouble ; I can walk with an ease that is surprising to myself. The India-Rubber Foot is, in my opinion, the next thing to life itself, obviating the necessity of an ankle-joint.

I have used other Artificial Legs that had ankle-joints, heel-cords, &c., that were clacking, breaking, and making a noise very obnoxious to the ear of one who has the misfortune to be mutilated. I take this opportunity to say to those who have met the missiles of the late unhappy war, that the inventions of A. A. Marks, 575 Broadway, New York, excel everything of the kind that I have ever met with in the way of substitutes for a lost limb.

Yours, very truly,
B. T. HUMPHREYS.

[LEG BELOW KNEE.]

CADDO, CHOCTOW NATION, INDIAN TERRITORY,
February 21st, 1876.

MR. A. A. MARKS:

Dear Sir:—It affords me pleasure, to be able to testify to the merits of your leg.

In 1864, I received a Government Leg, made by———. After wearing it a few months, I was compelled to have it cut off below the knee, and made over all below, in which condition I managed, with the assistance of a Peg Leg, to get along until the winter of 1866, when I had a new one made by another manufacturer, which worked very well for a few months, after which it was a continual source of annoyance ; I was compelled to send it for repairs at least three times, besides the tinkering I could do myself.

In 1870, I made application for a Government Leg of your make, with Rubber Foot, and can truthfully say that up to that time, I never dare leave home for any length of time, without taking my crutch or Peg Leg along.

I have worn your leg over five years continually with entire satisfaciton, doing a veriety of work, such as superintending a saw mill, Check Clerk and Express Agent : often carying 100 lbs. and upward. You now have my Government order for a new one, which I shall come for as soon as I can find time to come after it.

Yours respectfully,
ISRAEL W. STONE,
Formerly Co. M, First Illonois Artillery.

[LEG BELOW KNEE.]

MILLERTON, NEW YORK.
February 18th, 1876.

MR. A. A. MARKS:

Dear Sir :—When it gets so I cannot tell I am wearing an Artificial Leg (unless my attention is called to it) and use it as I would a natural one in jumping, playing ball, dancing, skating &c., in reference to Artificial Legs, I would have no others than your make. I have used the one I now have for over three years, through thick and thin, and can do a hard days work at anything, walk five or six miles and not feel any more fatigued than I would if I had both sound legs. I know several wearing your limbs, and all agree with me ; they are not complaining about the jar, as I have heard persons wearing other limbs with hard feet.

You are at liberty to use my name as occasion requires, for a reference.

Yours truly,
GEO. C. SMITH,
Telegraph Operator.

[LEG BELOW KNEE.]

WINONA, MINNESOTA.
February 24th 1876.

MR. A. A. MARKS:

Dear Sir :—I can hardly find words to express myself in regard to the Artificial Limb I purchased of you. *I like it.* I can't help but like it, and I have seen many others who wear your make of limbs, and they are *all* in the same fix. THEY LIKE THEM TOO. I am on the road most all of the time and see men wearing all kinds, and after they are worn a short time there is a noise that attracts attention. The *clap* of the foot and *rattle* of the ankle joint, that is where the Rubber Foot has the advantage over all others ; the sound of the step imitates the natural foot very nearly and thus deceives the uninitiated very neatly. I can skate as well as the most of them, and I attend a great many balls, and dance as many times in an evening as those with two natural legs, and if I do say it, there is none in the city that can dance more fancy dances, than your humble servant.

DAVID L. MASON,
Late of Co. B, 38th Wis. Vol.

[LEG BELOW KNEE.]

CHARLESTON, SOUTH CAROLINA,
February 15th, 1876.

MR. A. A. MARKS :

Dear Sir :—Please allow me to say for publication in your pamphlet, that I have worn your Patent Artificial Leg since 1868, and it has done excellent service. No better evidence is needed than the fact of my recent purchase of a new one from you.

Yours truly,
J. W. SMYSER.

[LEG BELOW KNEE.]

HAMILTON, BUTLER CO., OHIO,
February 15th, 1876.

MR. A. A. MARKS:

Dear Sir :—I take great pleasure in saying to you that the Patent Artificial Leg made by you and furnished me on government account last year, gives entire satisfaction, and from what I know of other kinds, and from a use of yours for over ten years, I most cheerfully recommend it as every way superior to any in use.

Yours respectfully,
MARTIN SEIFORD.

[LEG BELOW KNEE.]

WEST RANDOLPH, VERMONT,
February 15th, 1876.

Mr. A. A. MARKS :

Dear Sir :—I am very much pleased with my new Artificial Leg, although I have not worn it much, for the one you made me over five years ago is perfectly good yet. I have had two legs of other makers before I tried yours, they were both very unsatisfactory. I wish for no better leg than yours with patent rubber foot.

Yours sincerely,
L. H. GOODRICH,
Late Co. B, 6th Vermont Vols.

[LEG BELOW KNEE.]

ORANGE, ESSEX CO., NEW JERSEY,
February, 1876.

MR. A. A. MARKS :

Dear Sir :—I wish to say, through your pamphlet, to all whom it may concern, that your Patent Artificial Leg proves to be the best after years of hard usage, and I know pretty well about the other kinds too, from wearing them.

Yours truly,
THOMAS J. SPRAWL,
Late Corporal Co. C, 12th Regt. N. J. Vols.

[LEG BELOW KNEE.]

ROCK RIDGE, COLORADO TERRITORY,
March 2d, 1876.

MR. A. A. MARKS :

Dear Sir :—Please accept a few lines from my hand. I have worn one of your legs for the last four years ; I find it durable and convenient ; have plowed, harrowed and mowed with it, and also done most all kinds of farm work. Have attended balls and danced with any of them. Am much pleased with it. Would not exchange it for any other kind I have ever used or seen.

I take much pains in recommending it as the best.

Yours truly,
JOHN A. CASE,

[LEG BELOW KNEE.]

VERGENNES, VERMONT, February 11th, 1876.

A. A. MARKS, ESQ. :

Dear Sir :—I take great pleasure in recommending the Artificial Leg of which you are the patentee, as, in my opinion, it is the best now in use. I have worn one of ——, lateral motion, and one of ——, but consider yours is altogether superior to them in every respect. The wonderful ease and naturalness of movement of your India-rubber Foot cannot be excelled or equalled.

Very truly yours,
SIDNEY M. SOUTHARD.

[LEG BELOW KNEE.]

NEWARK, NEW JERSEY, February 9th, 1876.

MR. A. A. MARKS:

Dear Sir :—It is with great pleasure I recommend your Patent Artificial Legs. Having used others with ankle motion, I am able to judge the difference and the advantages of your Patent Rubber Foot ; there is no rattling or breaking down in these. I have given yours nearly six years' trial, without cost of one cent, and in so doing have proved the real merits and great satisfaction it has given me. I have done all kinds of farm work on it with comparatively no difficulty, which is something worth talking about for one with a stump but two and one-quarter inches long, below the knee.

Yours respectfully,
STEPHEN B. ANDREWS.

[LEG BELOW KNEE.]

PITTSBURGH, PA., 74 Grand Street.
February 10th, 1876.

MR. MARKS:

Dear Sir :—After several years of experience in the use of your Patent Leg, as well as those of different other manufacturers, and after extensive observation and enquiries among wearers of Artificial Limbs, I most *earnestly* and *emphatically* recommend your Patent Legs with Rubber Feet as the safest, most convenient and durable in the United States.

Yours truly,
JOHN G. JAMES.

[LEG BELOW KNEE.]

NAPANEE, LANOX CO., ONT., CANADA,
February 15th, 1876.

MR. A. A. MARKS:

Dear Sir :—I am glad to have an opportunity of placing in your hands, for publication, my experience and views of your Patent Artificial Legs. My six years of constant labor and exercise on your Patent Limbs, after a few years of experience on other, and more complicated substitutes, tells me that yours is in all respects by far the best in every essential feature, and over 50 per cent. more durable. The Rubber Foot suits me and I want no other now.

Yours &c.,
J. P. HANLEY,
Agent Grand Trunk Railway, Napanee, Ont,

[LEG BELOW KNEE.]

CANAAN FOUR CORNERS, COLUMBIA CO., NEW YORK.
February 9th, 1876,

MR. A. A. MARKS:

Dear Sir :—Having worn one of your legs over five years, and after a thorough trial of another kind, I can safely say that yours is the best. Your Rubber Foot does away with that tormenting rattle and expense of repairs at the ankle. I cheerfully recommend yours as in every way preferable.

Respecfully yours,
CHARLES H. GROVES.

52

BOISE CITY, IDAHO TERRITORY.
March 4th, 1876.
MR. A. A. MARKS:

Dear Sir :—In giving my testimony upon the subject of Artificial Legs, will say that I was supplied in 1865, by——with a leg, which never gave me any comfort, and then broke down too, in less than two years, then it was so noisy too, even from the first, if I had to go on a side-walk or hall it sounded like a drove of mules going across a bridge. I purchased one of your make in 1868, with Rubber Foot, which fitted me well, and I am still wearing it, never being troubled with loose, flapping joints, or cords being out of repairs ; on the contrary, the foot has a firm, noiseless, natural movement, superior to all other Artificial Legs, second only to the natural one.

I have applied for another one and shall be on for it the last of the month.
Yours respectfully,
RICHARD McCLOY,
10th Regt. N. Y. Cav. Vol.

ARTIFICIAL ARMS.

Without making any pretense that Artificial Arms are in any sense equal in utility and usefulness to Artificial Legs, yet of their real and comparative merits, I submit the following testimony ; all can judge of its reliability.

From Hon. Ira Buckman, Member of Assembly.

MR. A. A. MARKS :

Dear Sir :—It was my unfortunate lot, in the month of May, 1863, to meet with an accident by which the amputation of my right arm became necessary. After being confined to my bed and room some eight months from the loss of my arm and other injuries received at the time, I was permitted to take a position with that large but unfortunate class of my fellow-beings, who, like myself, have lost a limb, and must be what is commonly called a *cripple*, the balance of our sojourn here ; yet, with all the fearful forebodings that are forced upon the cripple's mind, there is yet a " balm in Gilead." What the beacon light is to the home-ward bound mariner, are A. A. MARKS' Artificial Limbs to the unfortunate. To think that he can again pass in mixed assemblages of his fellow-citizens without being gazed upon or pointed at, or, what is still worse, to hear that harsh, but oft-repeated exclamation, "there is a cripple !"

I have not only worn your Artificial Arm, but have shaken hands with a gentleman and his wife, both of whom called on me repeatedly when my arm was amputated. Neither of them discovered that they had been shaking an Artificial Hand, nor did some dozen other intimate acquaintances recognise it, forgetting for the time being, from its natural appearance, the loss of my arm.

Your Artificial Limbs need no eulogy from me. They only need to be seen and applied to be appreciated by the unfortunate.

As a mechanic, it might be well to ask the question, where are the weak points in your limbs? After a careful examination I fail to find even one ; so compact, so light, so simple of construction, and yet so well calculated to perform all the various functions that art can do for which they were intended, that further remarks from me seem unnecessary.
Very truly yours,
IRA BUCKMAN,
145 South Fifth Street, Brooklyn, E. D., N. Y.

Artificial arm for amputation below the elbow, but so near the joint as to render the joint useless, therefore operating same as in case the amputation was *above* the elbow.

METHODIST BOOK CONCERN.
805 Broadway, NEW YORK CITY.
March 20th, 1876.

Agents—R. NELSON, D. D.   J. M. PHILIPS.

Mr. A. A. MARKS:

Dear Sir :—Over four years constant use of your Patent Artificial Arm with Rubber Hand, and by prior experience for several years of other kinds, enables me to bear testimony to both the good qualities of yours and its superiority to others. It serves every useful purpose that any other can serve, and in wearing it I am not annoyed by the sensation, awakened by a noisy, clattering machine, or a rigid, unwieldy wooden hand. The Rubber Hand is much more agreeable, while its soft flexible substance much more nearly resembles a natural hand.

Very truly yours,

R. NELSON.

[ARM, BELOW ELBOW.]

MOUNT STERLING, MADISON CO., OHIO.
January, 1869.

A. A. MARKS, Esq. :

Dear Sir :—I have been wearing the Artificial Arm which you made for me in February, 1864, ever since the first day I got it, with the very best of success. I think it is the best arm made for utility and convenience, for the reason that it is so simple in construction. It will never get out of repairs, because there is so little machinery about it, and to all who wish to get an arm that has practical utility as well as neatness, I would certainly recommend your patent.

Yours respectfully,

S. B. YEOMAN,
Late Colonel 43d Reg't Col'd Tooops.

[ARM, BELOW ELBOW.]

SHERWOOD, CAYUGA CO., NEW YORK,
May 7th, 1865,

MR. A. A. MARKS:

Dear Sir :—I seat myself to inform you how I am getting along with my Artificial Arm, which you made me. Really, I am doing so well with it that I don't know in what particular point to speak. I am at work on the farm, as I used to do before the war, doing all kinds of work, such as plowing, sowing, and everything. In fact, your hook arrangement is just the thing for a farmer, and I do so much more with it generally, that it more than gives *good* satisfaction.

Truly yours,
BENJAMIN F. GOULD.
Late Private Co. 1, 3d New York Vols,

54

[ARM, BELOW ELBOW.]

NEW HAMBURGH, DUTCHESS CO., NEW YORK,
February 10th, 1876.

Mr. MARKS :

Dear Sir :—I have used the apparatus you made me for my arm, and find it a great benefit, and would not be without it at any price for hard work. It is a great benefit for working with long handled tools, such as shovels, spades, forks, &c. I can work with ease, and do as much as I ever could. Handling large bales, 400 to 500 lbs., I find it a great help to me ; also, in driving ; and if my arm was longer below the elbow, I should be able to do still better.

Yours truly,
WILLIAM SHAY.

[ARM, BELOW ELBOW.]

KELAMAZOO, MICH., 137 Main Street,
February 14th, 1876.

MR. A. A. MARKS :

Dear Sir :—I most cheerfully recommend your Artificial Hand as being the best I ever used. Have worn the one I now have for twelve years ; it never gets out of order.

Yours truly,
H. S. PARKER.

** [ARM, BELOW ELBOW.]

Office of JAMES H. GOLDEN,
County Clerk and Register of Deeds,
MAINSTEE, MICHIGAN,
March 1st, 1876.

MR. A. A. MARKS:

Dear Sir :—I ordered a hand of you in 1872, and must say that I am well pleased with it. It has done good service, and is good yet ; has cost nothing for repairs. I would not part with it if I could not get another.

I remain, as ever, yours truly,
JAMES H. GOLDEN.

NOTE.—It will be observed that the names of other makers alluded to in the letters, published herewith, are left blank, this is done, not by the desire of the writers, but as the publisher does *not* wish to disparage the work of any competitor in this calling by this publicity (no matter how high or how low their standing may be), thus keeping their names from the many thousand readers of this pamphlet, but in consideration of his duty to himself and to those who feel themselves victims of having a troublesome and unreliable substitute fastened upon them by the adroit exhibition of highly finished frail *jumping jacks*, in the shape of Artificial Limbs, as embellished by ingenious and fascinating words, will not refuse to give these names to individuals when privately requested, neither will he conceal the numerous and various specimens of Limbs left at his office by those who have renewed their *understandings* upod a firm, reliable and more satisfactory basis.

The following certificate and extended list of signatures thereto, is apparently superfluous, in addition to the already long list of recommendatory letters, &c., already printed in the preceding pages, but it must be borne in mind that patrons of this line of art are scattered widely apart, and all over the wide world ; they are generally very desirous of seeing some one using an Artificial Limb, if possible, before purchasing, and in order to place every possible means of reliable information in my power, in the hands of those seeking relief from lost limbs, and wishing to purchase, I have given an opportunity to some of my patrons to assist me and at the same time assist their-fellow unfortunates who do not possess that knowledge in thus securing the most reliable information that is possible to be had with the least possible trouble and in a form not to be mistaken ; as is fully and clearly shown by the long list of names, signed in every case by their own hands to the following

CERTIFICATE.

THE UNDERSIGNED respectfully state that they are now using and have used for a reasonable time, Marks' Patent Artificial Limbs, and are aware that the leading features in their mode of construction consists in the INDIA RUBBER FEET and HANDS, and are made with no movable ankle or finger joints, and *without* the complication of bolts, cords, springs, screws, &c., formerly used in Artificial Limbs ; the *Elastic* Feet and Hands being substitutes for the joints. And, FURTHERMORE, we also state that we have used other kinds and makers' limbs, WITH the joints, cords, &c., and from our experience with the different kinds, we cheerfully bear testimony that the Patent Artificial Limbs made by Mr. Marks, are in *no respect* inferior on account of their noted simplicity of construction, in dispensing with the joints, etc., but, on the other hand, we find in them a great relief from the cares and annoyances attending the complicated styles, and find that we experience greater *ease, comfort, elasticity, stillness, safety, and naturalness*, with these than with the other kinds, and also demonstrate the important fact that they are at least *one hundred per cent.* more durable than any other form of constructed limbs we have ever used, or have any knowledge of ; and recommend them most earnestly to all requiring Artificial Limbs, as the BEST.

MAJOR M. F. WATSON, 5th Artillery, U. S. A. (Retired), Montrose, Cumberland Co., Maryland. *Leg, above knee.*

**MR. SIMEON GILLIS, Recorder, Bryan, Williams Co., Ohio. *Leg, below knee.*

" FREDERICK LARRANAGA, Lima, Peru. *Leg, above knee.*

" GEO. W. GRAHAM, Post Master, Rushford, Filmore Co., Minn. *Leg, knee bearing.*

" AZARIAH A. GRANT, East Arlington, Vermont. *Leg, below knee.*

REV. ALFRED BLAKE, Gambier, Knox Co., Ohio. *Leg, above knee.*

MR. HIRAM J. CLARK, Insurance Agent, Binghamton, New York. *Leg, above knee.*

" D. B. WALKINGTON, Merchant, Belfast, Ireland. *Leg, above knee.*

** " J. C. SWITZER, Iowa National Bank, Iowa City, Iowa. *Leg, knee bearing.*

CAPT. ROBERT CATLIN, Co. D, 5th Regt. U. S. Artillery (Retired), West Point, New York. *Leg, below knee.*

MR. WILLIAM J. SMALLWOOD, Beatyville, Lee Co., Kentucky. *Leg, below knee.*

" JOHN McGUIRE, 31 Grand Ave., Brooklyn, N. Y. *Leg, below knee.*

" W. D. BRENNAN, late Capt. 124th Regt. N. Y. Vols. *Leg, below knee.*

" JOHN S. BIRD, Harrall, Decatur Co., Georgia. *Leg, below knee.*

** " E. B. EDDY, Bank President, Plainview, Wabashau Co., Minn. *Arm, below elbow.*

" F. W. HARNEY, Jersey City Ferry, New Jersey. *Leg, above knee.* ·

" TIMOTHY O'BRIEN, Binghampton, N. Y. BOTH LEGS, *below knee.*

" J. W. FARNSWORTH, Worcester, Mass. *Leg, below knee.*

" WILLIAM WICK, 262 Railroad Ave., Jersey City, New Jersey. *Leg, below knee.*

" DAVID M. GREEN (Post Master), Clayville, Oneida Co., New York. *Leg, knee bearing.*

" W. H. PACE, Railroad Agent, Communipaw, N. J. *Leg, below knee.*

" C. F. SCUDDER, Merchant, Binghamton, New York. *Leg, below knee.*

" ARTHUR T. COLBURN, East Somerville, Middlesex Co., Mass. *Leg, below knee.*

DR. T. W. WEEKS, No. 11 North 10th Street, Phila. Pa. *Leg, knee bearing.*

**MR. DANIEL MEAGHER, Machinist, 46 N Street, Sacramento City, Cal. *Leg, below knee.*

**REV. GEORGE BOSLEY, Cayuga Falls, Summit Co., Ohio. *Arm, below elbow.*

MR. JOHN G. POTTS, Printer, 181 Clinton Street, New York City. *Leg, below knee.*

" CHARLES A. FAAS, Jeweler, Plainville, Norfork Co., Mass. *Leg, below knee.*

" J. C. BUXTON, Grand Central Depot, N. Y. City. *Leg, above knee.*

" JAMES SHELL, Carters Depot, Carter Co., Tenn. *Leg below knee.*

" JOSEPH A. PETTET, Glenbulah, Sheboygan Co., Wisconsin. *Leg, below knee.*

" GASPER GEIST, Detroit, Michigan. *Arm, below elbow.*

Mr. ABRAM D. CLARK, No. 10 Tallman Street Brooklyn, New York.
Leg, above knee.

" EDGAR B. STEELE, Carthage, Jefferson Co., N. Y. *Leg, below knee.*

" J. H. GUNTHER, Hinton, West Virginia. *Leg, below knee.*

" PLINY P. LAIRD, Palmyra, Wayne Co., N. Y. *Leg, below knee.*

** " D. W. PRITCHARD, Delaware, Delaware Co., Ohio. *Leg, above knee.*

" HENRY BILLMAN, Van Wert, Van Wert Co., Ohio. *Leg, below knee.*

" MORRIS CHARTIERS, Beaver Creek, Cloud Co., Kansas. *Leg, below knee.*

" JOSIAH DURAN, Auburn, Maine. *Leg, above knee.*

" JOHN S. BRANNON, Glenville, Gilmer Co., West Virginia. *Leg, below knee.*

" H. A. BROTTS, Seville, Medina Co., Ohio. *Leg, below knee.*

" LEANDER A. ROBB, Burgettstown, Pa. *Leg, below knee.*

" B. M. LAMPMAN (Patent Roofing), Rutland, Rutland Co., Vt. *Leg, below knee,*

" SMITH B. PRITCHARD, Waterbury, Conn. BOTH LEGS, *below knees.*

" JACOB G. SHIRK, Chambersburgh, Penn. *Leg, below knee,*

" RICHARD O'KEEFE, Nat'l Home, Augusta, Maine. *Leg, below knee.*

" JOHN CAVANAUGH, Platteville, Grant Co., Wis. *Leg, below knee.*

" EDWARD BARRY, Punxatawney, Jefferson Co., Pa. *Leg, above knee.*

" W. H. DENISTON, Van Wert, Van Wert Co., Ohio. *Leg, below knee.*

" JOHN D. SMITH, Rockford, Winebego Co., Ills. *Leg, below knee.*

" DANIEL W. FOOT, Waterloo, Iowa. *Leg, below knee.*

" P. McCARTY, Contractor, Bergen Street, between Carlton and Vanderbilt Aves., Brooklyn. *Leg, below knee.*

" GEO. F. DRESSOIR, Felts Mill, Jefferson Co., N. Y. *Leg, below knee.*

" HENRY AUZBURGER, Machinist, 56 Van Brunt Street, Brooklyn, New York. *Leg, below knee.*

" EDWARD COLE, Merchant, Lexington, Green Co., New York. *Leg, knee bearing.*

" JOHN W. MERSHON, Cabinet Maker, Waverly Leuzerne Co., Penn. *Leg, below knee.*

" NORRIS CHAMBERLAIN, Farmer, Pelham, Hampshire Co., Mass. *Leg, below knee.*

" AUGUST WANDREY, Madison, Wisconsin. *Leg, below knee.*

" RUFUS TILBEE, Matteawan, Dutchess Co., N. Y. *Leg, below knee.*

" RODERICK GRAHAM, Printer, 13 Clinton Street, Brooklyn, N. Y. *Leg, above knee.*

" RORERT MARTIN, 741 East 6th Street, N. Y. City. *Leg, below knee.*

" CYRUS D. RIDENOUER, Hagerstown, Maryland. *Leg, below knee.*

" JOHN ASHELMAN, New Philadelphia, Pa. *Leg, below knee.*

" WILLIAM GRIFFIN, 1632 Sixteenth Street, N. W., Washington, D. C. *Leg, above knee,*

" FREDERICK H. BENNETT, Georgetown, Fairfield Co., Connecticut. *Leg, below knee.*

**Hon. T. ROBB, Deyerman, Dawson's Station, Feyette County, Penn. *Leg, below knee.*

Mr. WARREN BAKER, Worcester, Mass. *Leg, below knee.*

" AARON BYINGTON, Somerville, New Jersey. *Leg, below knee.*

** " CHRISTIAN MAY, Watertown, Dodge Co., Wis. *Leg, below knee.*

" R. B. ETHEREDGE, Rutledge, Morgan Co., Georgia. *Leg, below knee.*

" LEWIS JONES, South Norwalk, Conn. *Leg, above knee.*

** " H. D. CLARK, Humboldt, Nebraska. *Leg, below knee.*

" CHARLES A. SARGENT, Copperas Hill, Vermont. *Leg, below knee.*

** " JOHN McCLASKEY, Recorder, Toledo, Tama County, Iowa. *Leg, above knee.*

" CHARLES H. ROGERS, 25 Debevois Place, Brooklyn, New York. *Leg, below knee.*

" JOHN C. O'BRYAN, Marietta, Lancaster Co., Pa. *Leg, below knee.*

** " PETER PAULSON, Harness Maker, Rushford, Filmore Co., Minn. *Leg, above knee.*

" WILLIAM CLOSS, Black River, Jefferson Co., N. Y. *Leg, below knee.*

** " P. M. FAIREY, Branchville, Orangeberg Co., S. C. *Leg, below knee.*

" S. F. FELLOWS, Athens, Bradford Co., Pa, *Leg, above knee.*

** " THOMAS FIELDSON, 612 N. 4th St., St. Louis, Mo. *Leg, below knee.*

" D. M. JONES, Alderman, Hyde Park, Luzerne County, Pa. *Leg, above knee.*

** " LUTHER LUCORE, Farmer, Benzette, Elk Co., Pa. *Leg, below knee.*

" WILLIAM MILLER, Clarkstown, Rockland Co., New York. *Leg, below knee.*

** " ELLIS HUMPHREY, Book Keeper, Middle Granville. Washington Co., N. Y. *Leg, above knee.*

" WILLIAM HARVEY, Tippecanoe, Fayette Co., Pa. *Leg, below knee.*

** " JOHN A. CRAWFORD, Harness Maker, Masonville, Delaware Co., New York *Leg, above knee.*

" PHILEMON CAYWOOD, Lindley, Grundy Co., Mo. *Leg above knee.*

** " ROBERT TAGGERT, Wheeling, Cook Co.. Ill. *Leg, above knee.*

" E. A. TILLOTSON, Lancing, Michigan, *Leg, below knee.*

Mrs. ANGELINE FLEEZER, Marbledale, Litchfield Co., Connecticut. *Leg, abov knee.*

Mr. JAMES BOYLE, 43 Grand Street, Brooklyn, E. D., New York. *Leg, below knee.*

" H. R. HORSFORD, Hudson, New York. *Leg, below knee.*

" E. D. SCOFIELD, Passaic, Passaic Co., New Jersey. *Leg, above knee.*

** " Mrs. AGATHA KRUGER, Albion, Jackson Co., Wis. *Leg, below knee.*

Mr. JOHN BRANDT, 197 Broadway, New York. *Leg, above knee.*

** " J. F. PRIOR, Northfield, Rice Co., Minn. *Leg, below knee.*

" JOSEPH C. STEVENS, Bloomfield, Essex Co., New Jersey. *Leg, above knee.*

** " JOHN H. BURNHAM, Amity, Yomhill Co., Oregon. *Leg, below knee.*

" GEORGE D. STINEBAUGH (County Clerk), Franklin Co., Kansas. *Leg, below knee.*

**Mrs. S. A. LINDER, Eugene City, Lane Co., Oregon. *Leg, above knee.*

Mr. HUGH McANULTY, Painter, Bay Shore, Suffolk Co., New York. *Leg, below knee.*

" WILLIAM R. RALPH, Engineer, 162 Prince Street, New York City. *Leg, above knee.*

** " J. L. COLE, Green, Butler Co., Iowa. *Leg, below knee.*

" GEORGE W. McDOUGAL, Newark, New Jersey. *Leg, knee bearing.*

** " JEREMIAH KEADY, Blacksmith, cor. Cook and Tremont Streets, Baltimore, Maryland. *Leg, above knee.*

" GEORGE W. KENYON, Hebron, Potter Co., Pa. *Leg, below knee.*

** " WOODAL EASTMAN, Farmer, South Atselic, Chenango Co., New York. *Leg, above knee.*

" WM. M. WHITE, Farmer, Williamson, Wayne Co., New York. *Leg, above knee.*

" REUBEN HALL, Oil City, Pa. *Leg, below knee.*

** " JACOB PALMERTER, Collector of Customs, Plattsburgh, Clinton Co., New York. *Leg, knee bearing.*

" JOSEPH L. STEELE, Cherry Creek, Arapahoe Co., Colorado Territory. *Leg, below knee.*

**Mrs. MATILDA REED, Vinton, Benton Co., Iowa. *Leg, above knee,*

Mr. WILLIAM H: HAMLIN, Indianapolis, Ind. *Leg, above knee.*

" MICHAEL R. HOGAN, Meriden, Conn. *Leg, below knee.*

" CHAS. R. KASMIRE, New Bedford, Mass. *Leg, below knee.*

" FREDERICK J. LAWRENCE, Wood Haven, Queens Co., New York. *Leg, above knee.*

" JAMES H. KYNER, Norfolk, Nebraska. *Leg, below knee.*

* " JAMES W. BARNES, Farmer, Louisville, Blount Co., Tennessee. *Leg, above knee.*

" DAVID L. MASON, Winona, Minn. *Leg, below knee.*

Mrs. ALFRED ROBERTS, New Dorp, New York. *Leg, knee bearing.*

Mr. THOMAS R. GIBSON, 37 Ritch Street, San Francisco, California. *Leg, below knee.*

" ANDREW JOHNSON, Branchville, New Jersey. *Leg, below knee.*

** " R. E. LAWHON, Atlanta, Georgia. *Leg, below knee.*

" WILLIAM DORNSCHEIDTE, 47 Adams Street, Brooklyn, New York. *Leg, below knee.*

" JOSEPH HENNENLOTTER, 460 Court Street, Brooklyn, New York. *Leg, above knee.*

" WILLIAM WORTS, Brooklyn, E. D., New York. *Leg, below knee.*

" CHRISTOPHER HAFFERN, 273 Tenth Avenue, New York City, *Leg, below knee.*

** " REUBEN A. HEALEY, Cross Mills, Charlestown, Rhode Island. *Leg, below knee.*

" EDWARD A. NELLIS, Winstead, Conn. *Leg. below knee.*

" CHARLES McDOWELL, Clayville, Oneida Co., New York. *Leg, above knee.*

** " CHARLES GUMMELL, Calverton, Baltimore, Md. *Leg, below knee,*

" RICHARD CLEARWATER, Newport, Vermillion Co., Indiana. *Leg, below knee.*

** " H. C. CARVER, Farmer, College Springs, Page Co., Iowa. *Leg, below knee.*

" ALBERT HAUSBECK, 156 Green St. Jersey City, N. J. *Leg, below knee.*

" JOSEPH TROW, 605 Fifth Avenue, N. Y. City. *Leg, above knee.*

" E. E. BACON, Rochelle, Ogle Co., Illinois. *Leg, below knee.*

" JOHN SEEREY, Bridgeport, Conn. *Leg, above knee.*

" GEO. F. BAILEY, Jeweler, 11 Maiden Lane, New York City. *Leg, above knee.*

:* " LYMAN H. NORRIS, Barrington, Yates Co., Y. Y. *Leg, below knee.*

" A. B. HOWELL, Lawyer, Eastern, Pennsylvania. *Leg, above knee.*

" JOHN FITZGERALD, Front St., Newburgh, Orange Co., N. Y. *Leg, below knee.*

** " F. McGUIRE, Farmer, Jacksonville, Chickasaw County, Iowa. *Leg, below knee.*

" WALTER S. KANE, 30 Broad St., New York City. *Leg above knee.*

" JOSEPH LOMAS, Collector, Newburgh, Orange Co., New York. *Leg, below knee.*

** " ABRAM S. MORRIS, 924 C Street, Washington, D C. *Leg, above knee.*

" D. S. HERMANCE, R. R. Agt., Hemstead Queens Co., N. Y. *Leg, below knee.*

" WM. FRANCIS, Holland Patent, Oneida Co., N. Y. *Leg, knee bearing.*

" D. E. ISHAM, Westfield, Cattaraugus Co., N. Y. *Leg, below knee.*

" JAS. S. McDANOLDS, State Librarian, Trenton, N.J. *Leg, knee bearing*

:* " JOHN KENNADY, Mountain Lake, Minn. *Leg, below knee.*

" CUTLE H. RIST, West branch, Richmond Co., Wis. *Leg, above knee.*

** " ANTHONY BERTRAND, Merced Falls, California. *Arm below elbow.*

" DAVID HERSHBERG, 154 Attorney St., N. Y. City, *Leg, below knee.*

** " WILSON, ANDREW W., Marysville, Yuba Co., Cal. *Leg, knee bearing.*

" BEERI SERVISS, Apple River, Jo Davises Co., Ills. *Leg, below knee.*

** " HENRY SMITH, Apple River, Jo Davises Co., Ills. *Leg, abov knee.*

" A. L. RUSHMORE, Conneautville, Crawford County, Pennsylvania. *Leg, above knee.*

" JOSEPH Y. PAXTON, McPherson, Kansas. *Leg, below knee.*

The Press has spoken of these Limbs in flattering and very complimentary terms on many occasions, but find room only for the following articles at this time:

From the *American Eclectic Medical Review*, Aug., 1866.

MARKS' PATENT ARTIFICIAL LIMBS.

These Limbs are beyond all question the most perfect and simple ever made, and their indorsement by the American Institute at its last Annual Fair was but a just tribute to their unquestionable excellence. The principle . of the India Rubber Feet and Hands *is the true one;* and the remarkable skill and extensive experience of Dr. Marks in this branch of surgical appliances is unexcelled in this country OR THE WORLD.

We recommend Marks' Artificial Limbs—unqualifiedly—to *all* surgeons and to all who may require the aid of such appliances.

ARTIFICIAL LEGS ON SKATES.

[The following communication is handed in by a friend, in whose knowledge of the facts we have full confidence. We have frequent inquiries in regard to the manufacturers of Artificial Limbs, and we deem any facts in relation to them interesting to disabled men. We witnessed the walking match refered to by our correspondent, and from the testimony of those who have used both the Ordinary Limbs and the Rubber Feet, we imagine that the latter would become a favorite.—ED. SOLDIER'S FRIEND.]

The time has not long passed since it was considered a wonder to see a person walking with apparent ease upon one Artificial Leg, but when an unfortunate fellow who had lost both of his propellers was enabled to walk, even with two canes, it was thought so remarkable that few would *believe* it without witnessing the feat with their own eyes, But we have recently seen something far exceeding this in novelty and success. We saw a young man *skating* leisurely along on the Central Park Lake, with both hands in his pockets, and without any assistance of staff or cane. It is true he did not carve out with exquisite neatness and precision, an elegantly spread eagle, neither did he leap over the heads of his fellow skaters, but his movements were easy and graceful, and no one would suspect any thing unusual, except that he might be a beginner. This was really the case, as he had then put on skates only a few times. Our attention was called to him by some one who knew him personally, or we should not have thought that among that vast throng there was one who sought the merry sport upon *two wooden legs.* We should not call them wooden, for the quiet skater was no less a personage than Mr. Frank Stewart, who wears the Artificial Legs with Rubber Feet, invented and manufactured by Mr. Marks, 575 Broadway, in this city. Mr. Stewart ran, or walked, the race at the Fair of the American Institute last year, and made the unprecedented time of half a mile in nine minutes, with no assistance whatever, and was still anxious to proceed declaring he could make the next half mile in the same time, but was prevented by the crowd.

The Gold Medal for Artificial Limbs, was awarded to Mr. Marks, at the American Institute Fair, 1865.—*Soldier's Friend, January*, 1866.

The *American Phrenological Journal* of October, 1869, published a lengthy and comprehensive article on *Artificial Limbs*, from which will be found the following extract and engraving of Mr. Stewart:

ARTIFICIAL LIMBS.

It is but a few years since the person who was unfortunate enough to lose a part of his leg, was obliged to stump about, like poor "Tommy Taft," in Mr. Beecher's "Norwood," for the rest of his life, or, what was worse, to swing himself through the world on crutches.

There have been various ingenious and useful devices to obviate the old stump-leg, as well as to do away with the crutches, and these inventions have served their purposes with more or less convenience and pleasure to the wearer and his friends.

Since the beginning of our great rebellion ten thousand maimed soldiers have called upon the inventive talent of our citizens, and now we have the pleasure of presenting, for the consideration of our readers, the Artificial Limbs with India-rubber Hands and Feet, invented and manufactured by Mr. A. A. Marks, 575 Broadway, New York.

We give also an engraved likeness of Mr. Frank Stewart, who has had both legs amputated below the knees, and wears, of course, two artificial legs. One amputation is within two and a half inches of the knee-joint, the other five or six inches below it, yet with his two artificial legs he walks very briskly and very much better than many men having corns, who would resent the imputation of being lame. The dotted lines across the legs show where the amputations were made. He uses a cane, but can walk without it.

We see nothing in the artificial line which gives so natural a step as this.

We are informed that Mr. Marks has been authorized to furnish artificial Limbs, at the expense of the Government, to commissioned officers, soldiers and seamen of the United States army and navy, who may have been maimed in the service of their country. It is a source of great pleasure to us, and must be to everybody, that the maimed soldier, without special charity from personal friends, should thus be enabled to procure, at no expense to himself, the BEST POSSIBLE SUBSTITUTE for the limbs which he has sacrificed for the honor and freedom of his country.

We recommend all persons who are interested to make an investigation for themselves of this work, and we doubt not they would be pleased and profited thereby.

From the *New York Dispatch*, September 16, 1866.

ARTIFICIAL LIMBS.—In another column of this paper the reader will find an advertisement under the above heading. These Artificial Limbs are the invention and manufacture of A. A. Marks, Esq., of No. 575 Broadway, this city. We have seen some of these limbs, and examined the peculiar simplicity of their construction ; we have also seen them in practical use, and have been truly astonished with the naturalness and grace with which they walk. They remind us of the great advance made in the steam-engine by being shorn of its former and many complicated parts, to its present simple and improved condition. Mr. Marks *dispenses* with the ANKLE *joints* in his legs and its COMPLICATIONS, by substituting a foot made mostly of *India-Rubber*, of a very tough, elastic and desirable character, thereby giving the wearer a more *reliable*, *natural* and *perfect* limb than we have heretofore ever seen.

At the Fair of the American Institute last year, there was a very spirited contest for the Gold Medal to be awarded to the inventor of the best limb, and although there were many contestants, Mr. Marks' limbs carried off the prize.

Mr. Marks is a *pioneer* in this line of *art* having been engaged in his profession for the last fifteen years, and after much study and many experiments has attained to those special improvements, which he patented some *four* years since. The government some time since adopted his limbs, thus enabling our heroic soldiers who have lost their limbs in defence of their country, to secure them free of charge.

We have given these inventions more than a *passing* notice, as we think they effect *important* changes and improvements in the construction of implements for the relief of our unfortunate fellow beings, and more especially as they emanate from one who has labored for many years in this branch of a noble work, and whose present standing as an *inventor* and *gentleman* needs no further recommendation at our hands.

The following Editorial Notice appeared in the *New York Tribune* of September 16th, 1868.

ARTIFICIAL LIMBS.

The inventor who can make a machine to do its work with the least machinery is considered by all good judges as the best. Simplicity of construction, in everything, is not only its beauty, but its best recommendation. In nothing is this rule more applicable than to substitutes for lost limbs, especially when applied to our brave soldiers and seamen, who sacrificed their own precious limbs to save our country.

We find the above qualifications well exemplified in Artificial Limbs invented and manufactured by A. A. Marks, 575 Broadway, which seem to combine every feature of utility and comfort to the unfortunate wearer, while their simplicity of construction must render them durable and unlikely to get out of order. The soldier or citizen who places himself under the care of Mr. Marks will find a competent, prompt and reliable friend, a man well known as an energetic, hard worker, of large experience as an inventor and mechanic in a profession both honorable and beneficial to the human race. He publishes a pamphlet descriptive of his productions, which he sends free to all applicants.

The *New York Dispatch*, of October 24, 1869, contained the following Editorial notice which is here reprinted verbatim:

Very few persons in proportion to our population, are required to use Artificial Limbs, yet in looking into the matter a little, we find there are many thousands among us, needing and using those useful inventions of art, and many persons use them with such ease and naturalness, that their misfortune is never known by the public, and often but by very few of their acquaintances. In examining Mr. Marks' large case of Artificial Limbs at the Fair, our attention was attracted to a very genteel and pretty little girl of about ten years of age, who presented us with a card which read : "A. A. Marks' Patent Artificial Limbs, 575 Broadway, New York," and upon the opposite side we found a portrait of the little girl above mentioned, taken in different positions, one of which represented her as she appeared before me with her sweet, honest face and lovely black eyes, and skipping about apparently as sound in limb as in body and mind, but another view represented her sitting and exhibiting her misfortune, showing that her left leg was amputated just below the knee. She informed us that she had used it for over two years, and with perfect ease. We saw her afterward walking about the Fair without exhibiting any signs whatever of her loss. We are informed that Mr. Marks has hundreds of patients who testify to the great utility and assistance they receive from his valuable inventions—many, too, who have lost both legs, and with these substitutes are enabled to attend to their vocations. These limbs took the first premium in 1865 and 1867, and will, beyond doubt, do the same this year. His cases of limbs are constantly attended by some one wearing either one or two of these substitutes, and attract a large share of interest at the Exhibition.

From the *Illustrated Weekly*, New York, Dec. 18, 1875.

We have been particularly interested in reading a pamphlet issued by A. A. Marks, No. 575 Broadway, New York, explaining the construction of the Artificial Limbs produced at his extensive factory, which must be placed at the head of all institutions of the kind on this continent.

Established in his business about twenty years, Mr. Marks has succeeded beyond expectation in the endeavor to produce the most perfect substitute possible for a lost limb, either arm or leg. All the limbs manufactured by him are light and strong, elastic and uncomplicated, and admit of such use as is perfectly wonderful. Persons wearing his legs—we intend no joke— find themselves able to walk long distances, to work in the fields or the store, and, in the case of ladies, to perform all their domestic duties, including going up and down stairs, without weariness and want of grace, so that their wearing artificial assistances of this nature may not be known to their associates. This is true even of persons necessitated to wear two Artificial Legs. The foot is of India Rubber—as are the hands made by Mr. Marks— light and elastic, and the joints are so constructed as to obviate noise and stiffness. It has been found that children from four years and upwards, wearing legs of Mr. Marks' manufacture, can indulge in their childish sports and grow up in vigorous health, instead of feebly moving by aid of crutches. We need not add that the inventor has achieved a brilliant success in his business, and that persons and institutions of eminence have cheerfully accorded their expression of the utility of his inventions, which those who have used them know best how to appreciate. We cordially indorse the verdict of the judges at the Forty-fourth Fair of the American Institute, lately held in this city : " We regard them (Mr. Marks' Artificial Limbs) as superior to all others in practical efficiency and simplicity." We may add that Mr. Marks has received numerous medals from the judges of this institution, the first dated as far back as 1859.

From the *Toledo Blade*, Toledo, Ohio, Aug. 26, 1875.

WONDERFUL IMPROVEMENTS IN PATENT ARTIFICIAL LIMBS.

The limbs manufactured at the establishment of DR. A. A. MARKS, 575 Broadway, New York, we are warranted in saying, from personal examination, are beyond any question the most perfect ever made, and their indorsement by the American Institute at its last annual Fair, was but a just tribute to their unquestionable excellence.

The principle of the India Rubber feet and hands *is the true one*, and the remarkable skill, and the twenty-two years' experience of DR. MARKS in this branch of surgical appliance, is simply unexcelled in this country or in THE WORLD. They are recommended and fully indorsed by all leading surgeons throughout this entire country.

GRAND ARMY RECORD—ARTIFICIAL LIMBS.

Science and the industrial arts present no higher evidence of progress than that observable in the perfection of surgical appliances designed to replace portions of the human form, removed by innumerable causes. The requirements of an article of this description are not only to come as near as possible to nature in appearance, but in the uses of the lost part. Take the leg for example. It should not only look the counterfeit of Nature ; but, its wearer must be able to walk, dance, run, skate, or do anything as before his misfortune, and at the same time have the limb conform to his person.

Of the truly ingenious and vastly useful devices for these purposes, examples have recently come under our notice, which show conclusively that the best articles of this description ever devised by man's ingenuity, and one which fully meets the requirements, is the Artificial Limbs, with India Rubber hands and feet, made by Dr. A. A. Marks, of this city, and which are now in such extensive use throughout the whole country. Consisting of the simplest conditions, availed of with most consummate ability, it is a model of elegance, naturalness, and efficiency, and fully deserve the high encomiums it has recived from medical and other scientific sources, from the Government, the press, and public generally.

Of course Dr. Marks' peculiar features in perfecting Artificial Limbs, are secured to him by letters-patent, and he is the sole manufacturer of them.

Those interested can send to his office or manufactory, No. 575 Broadway. New York City, and procure a work, gratuitously, which contains a full description of his products, testimonials from thousands who are now using them ; accounts of medals, diplomas, and other evidence of approbation awarded them. By a special Act of Congress, the Surgeon-General of the United States has commissioned Dr. Marks to supply these limbs to commissioned officers, soldiers, seamen and others, free of charge, under stripulated regulations. Those afflicted, or having friends deprived of their limbs, should communicate with Dr. Marks.

From the *Davenport Democrat*, Davenport, Iowa, February 10th, 1876.

SUBSTITUTED HUMANITY.

The imitation of portions of humanity with all those movements which which are peculiar to the substituted limb, has arrived at a perfection which is marvelous. The victim of patriotism or the sufferer from an accident who requires the amputation of a member can now be supplied with hand or foot, arm or leg so perfect in contour, and so elegant in action, that the sense of loss is reduced to a minimum. Especially is this the case with Marks' patents, which are made with rubber hands and feet so exactly *fac-simile* that none but the wearer is cognizant of the substitution.

Mechanical surgery, carried thus to perfection, ranks in importance with those other inventions and discoveries which have made America the leading nation of the world in the alleviation of suffering humanity. Disabled soldiers and citizens should apply at once to A. A. Marks, 575 Broadway, N. Y., for a descriptive catalogue published by him, which also contains instructions *how* to make application for the government supply of artificial limbs.

The *New York Evening Mail* of November 12th, 1875, in giving an account of the most prominent articles on exhibition at the American Institute Fair, alluded to this subject, as follows :

Undoubtedly, one of the most valuable features of the whole exhibition, is the display of Artificial Limbs, made by Dr. A. A. Marks, of 575 Broadway, New York.

The beautiful young lady who attends the case of goods entered by Dr. Marks, has been wearing one of his Artificial Limbs for the last eight years.

A photograph is distributed at the Fair, showing her as she was at the age of eight, and as she now appears, which very beautifully illustrates a specialty in his business in applying Artificial Limbs to children.

These limbs are constructed with India-rubber Hands and Feet, and are models of elegance, naturalness and efficiency ; in short, they are the best articles of this description ever devised by man's ingenuity. They are now in extensive use throughout the whole country, and have received the highest indorsements from medical and other scientific sources, from the government, the press, and the public generally.

An illustrated pamphlet, giving full description of the limbs, opinions of eminent surgeons, and testimonials of hundreds who are now using them, can be procured gratuitously by addressing as above.

The Editor of the *Stamford Advocate*, a large weekly newspaper of long and first-class standing, published at Stamford, Connecticut (a large, populous, rural town, thirty-three miles from New York City, on the New York, New Haven and Hartford Railroad), after paying us a hasty call on a recent occasion, gave an account of his visit in the editorial columns, which is here republished *verbatim et literatim :*

ART PRACTICALLY EXEMPLIFIED.

While on a visit to the city a short time since, we made a call at the celebrated manufactory of Artificial Limbs, owned and carried on by Mr. A. A. Marks, at 575 Broadway, and although we had known before something of this establishment, we were surprised to see and learn of the real extent and magnitude of what we had always before considered quite an insignificant business. Mr. Marks is, with but a single exception, the oldest manufacturer and inventor in the United States, in this line. He started in the business in a small way nearly a quarter of a century ago, and has gradually increased it until his patrons are numbered by the thousands, and are scattered in almost every part of the globe. While there, he showed us a fine specimen of a full length Artificial Leg made for a gentleman in Buenos Ayres, South America, for whom he had made one a few years ago, and he was so well pleased with it that he had again sent this long distance for a duplicate. Mr. M. showed us another for a young man in the northern part of California. One also for a Miss of twelve years old, who lost her limb by a mowing machine when she was but three. More than a dozen more were shown us either finished or in progress of construction, for persons of various occupations, and scattered widely over the world, some of a peculiar historic character. But more than this, he showed us the practical working of one particular case that was well worth seeing, He was a snugly built boy of eleven years of age. Mr. M. says : "Tommy, let the gentleman see you walk," upon which he started off without a cane, at an easy gait, with a slight limp in the right leg. We thought it excellent walking for any one with an Artificial Leg, and so expressed ourselves, supposing, of course, that he was wearing but one Artificial, but when informed that the solid little fellow was walking on a *pair* of Artificial Legs, and shown his photograph taken with his bare stumps, this told the story so clear that no doubt could be entertained of his actual condition, and that the little fellow had lost one leg just below the knee and the other above, and yet he walks well and for long distances without any cane. This case has excited much wonder and comment where the boy is known. Dr. Samuel Brady, of Brooklyn, has written a brief yet very concise account of this wonderful case. He amputated the limbs after the mutilation by the railroad cars.

Mr. M. then called our attention to a young man of about twenty-six years of age, who was walking about the large reception room, and informed us that he was wearing a pair of artificials also. From his easy manner and steady step none would for a moment suspect he was in any way disabled. This personage has been in Mr. M.'s employ for nearly a dozen years, therefore grown from a mere boy in an occupation which accident compelled him to patronize, and in which he steadily labors in assisting others who, from accident or disease, are similarly circumstanced.

The inventor was awarded a GOLD MEDAL for the BEST ARTIFICIAL LIMBS at the great Fair of the American Institute, in 1865, and also the *highest awards* of that time-honored institution at every exhibition since.

Mr. Marks has a peculiar faculty of making those who call on him feel interested in his humanitarian work. He certainly has developed this peculiar business to a wonderful extent. Many a brave soldier has had his life made happy by having his missing leg or arm replaced with one of Mr. Marks' artificial ones. The nation owes him a debt of gratitude for his untiring efforts in this department.

Mr. M. is a resident of Riverside. He lives on his fine farm on the banks of Long Island Sound, a short drive from our village, where his life and tastes are beautifully exemplified by his ornamental surroundings on the breezy shore. His orchards and well tilled grounds yield ample harvests. Thus he shows an ardent love for nature's quiet and pure attractions, as well as for the development of art in his singular though necessary profession.

Appleton's Journal of June 19th, 1875, contained the following article. It treats upon other subjects than Limbs, but *Artificial* is the theme, and it is so ably handled that the reader cannot help but be instructed as well as amused in its perusal.

PATCHED UP HUMANITY.

It is quite appalling how callous we have grown to the tendency of the fair sex to amplify Nature by artificial means. we no longer look upon Sophronia's mass of back-hair with suspicious dread. The most gallant of men, the weakest dupe of feminine arts, is not deceived by it ; nor does he suppose that it indicates any real deficiency as in the natural supply. He recognizes and sanctions it, not as a snare, but a graceful concession to fashion ; and the women themselves do not seek concealment.

I have watched fair girls—girls with sunshiny tresses waved across their brows, enter the store of a *perruquier* on Broadway without a blush—without a moment's care for observers—and I have seen them boldly comparing the shade of their cast-off, lack-lustre braids with new ones, which they have purchased under the very eyes of prying men.

The propriety of thus amending Nature whenever fashion demands, seems to be generally conceded, not only in the matter of hair, but also in many other things, and I am much too discreet a person to find fault with that which meets the approval of so many. I will go even so far as to say that it may be partly a good tendency, in the interest of candor and against deceit, for while the custom is extant it is surely better to be honest about it.

If Mrs. B——has the misfortune to be sallow, and finds her complexion improved by the use of anthosmimos, at two dollars a bottle, we should be glad that the pejudices of her neighbor do not compel the poor lady to be hypocritical over it ; and the understanding that Fanny's profusion of hair is not wholly her own will spare dear Edgar many a heart-pang after marriage.

But there is also a tendency to substitute as well as to amplify Nature. Formerly, a cripple was a cripple, and hobbled through the world an object of pity to sympathetic elders, and of derision to wicked youngsters. An unfortunate with one eye had no means of hiding his defect, and the loss of the arms made a person helpless. Even when artificial legs were first introduced, they were so imperfect that no one was deceived by them. They had movable, clattering ankle-joints, which betrayed their wearer at every step, and his entrance into a parlor was mistaken for the complaint of a broken-down chair, or the squeak of a rat. When he moved in the street, people turned round, expecting to see a wheelbarrow in want of grease approaching, and when—awful moment!—he cast himself on his knees before his adored one, his impassioned utterances were accompanied with rattling noises, which suggested the unrest of a fallen spirit in torment. Naughty little boys whistled the tune of the "Cork Leg" in his presence, and his whole life was made miserable by the rude queries of persons who wanted to know all about his misfortune.

Such improvements have been made in late years, however, that, in all but sense of touch, an artificial leg performs the most important duties of a natural one, allowing the wearer to walk, run, or sit with ease, and to endure an astonishing degree of fatigue in an upright position. It is noiseless, and only an expert can detect it.

The foot wears a real boot, which can be removed at pleasure ; the knee and ankle joints work without a creak, and the whole mechanism is, as one maker eloquently says, "at once a beauty and a joy forever." The form is perfection, the instep really arched, and the ankle-trim. The calf swells with exquisite gradations, and recedes toward a well-shaped knee. The surface is smooth and glossy as satin, and delicately tinged with a color between a soft pink and a luscious creaminess, as unlike the abnormal and offensive redness of a ballet-girl's fleshings as blush rose is unlike a flaunting dahlia.

A wooden leg, pure and simple, is a perpetual reminder of the wearer's bereft condition. It can never be mistaken for any thing more than the shallow mechanism it is. But the modern artificial leg is a complete illusion, and the wearer himself may easily forget its unreality. Coming home in the evening from a day of toil, and throwing himself into an arm-chair for a consoling smoke, he can take off his boots and put on his slippers in the most natural manner possible. His stockings—prosaic necessity—need changing once a week, and I have heard of men who gratified their inordinate vanity by clothing their rubber feet in the softest of silks. Then, if he be of a utilitarian turn, with little care for trappings and seemings, he can discard the limb altogether when he is seated, and put it in a corner like an umbrella or a walking-stick. Or, if he has the native habit of sitting with his heels elevated above his body, he can continue to enjoy that delusive pleasure by resting his artificial leg on the window-sill while he sits upon the lounge in a more comfortable posture. A thousand advantages suggest themselves, and therein we find an example of the excellent law of compensation which atones for so many of our grievances.

But, when we glance through the neck of the leg, so to speak, our feelings suffer a revulsion. We see that all the external beauty and tenderness, all the lustre and refinement of tint, only serve to hide a combination of ugly iron bolts, rods, and screws, which give the thing its movements.

The outer case or shell is made of wood, wrought by a carpenter's chisel, and when we rap it with our knuckles it gives fourth a hollow, sepulcharal sound. The delicate texture of the surface is the result of a coating of some kind of fine enameled leather, which makes the wood more durable and handsome, and prevents it from splitting or cracking. So the artificial leg æsthetic is dismissed from our minds, and we have only to consider the practical leg as a thing of mechanical ingenuity and utility.

Resting on a soft pad, the natural limb fits into the socket of the artificial, and the latter is held in its place by a strong elastic brace worn over the shoulders. The knee-joint is formed by a broad convex surface of the thigh-piece working in a corresponding concavity in the leg-piece, or *vice-versa*, and these articulating surfaces, as the manufacturer calls them, are held in position by a horizontal steel tube.

But we shall only involve the reader and ourselves in attempting to elucidate dry technicalities, and hence we shall leap to a more interesting part of the subject. We have seen what the artificial leg is ornamentally, and we have hinted at its possibilities, but we have given you no idea of how varied and extensive these possibilities are. We know a gentleman with a passion for pedestrianism, an excellent skater, who moves on two artificial legs, and yet this is nothing.

In a pamphlet before us there are several pages filled with the experiences of crippled men whose infirmities have been relieved, not by the all-potent grace of winking Madonnas, nor by the talismanic touch of sainted hands, but by the dexterity of artisans in human-repair shops.

A brevet major of United States Volunteers, who was cut in two during the war writes, "I walk six miles every day without a cane or other assistance." Another martyr of gunpowder declares, "I am employed in a locomotive-works, and with the aid of an artificial leg I am able to support a large family." Think of supporting a large family on an artificial leg, and dandling a baby on an artificial knee! And what a sermon and example it is to those who complain that they connot afford to marry with even the two natural limbs at their service! This is not all, however. "Being fond of sport, I have frequently started from home early in the morning and have not returned until night, spending the whole day in hunting-exploits, and accomplishing altogether about fifteen miles' distance." This same hero is member of a fire-department, and is often in active service. If you saw him in the street you could not discover his imperfections, for, beyond a slight limp, his gait is steady and easy.

Still another writes, "With my artificial leg I have visited the Highlands and all the noteworthy scenery of Ireland, Wales, England, Germany, France, and Switzerland, and have ever found it all I desired while on horse-back, on foot, or at rest."

A fourth states that he is a farmer, and that he has built a stone-fence while wearing an artificial leg, mowed and cradled, spread and pitched hay, and made himself generally useful.

We imagine that the wearers of these artificial limbs grow attached to them, as to a meerschaum pipe. and it occurs to us that there must be a large amount of satisfaction in taking one's leg off and rubbing it up and down in a fondling way. Some connoisseurs—for there are connoisseurs even in this—have collections of legs—week-day legs, Sunday-legs, dancing legs, and riding-legs, each expressly made for a distinct purpose. But this is vanity and leadeth only unto vexation of spirit.

Concluding we will speak of one other thing in the human-repair shops —the artificial eye, which has been brought to such a state of perfection by a French oculist of latter days that it effectually disguises the greatest defect. Formerly it never fitted well in the socket ; but now it exactly imitates the natural eye, and for fifty or a hundred dollars you can obtain a melting blue orb, a wistful gray, or a fiery black.

The New York Commercial Advertiser, Saturday, August 26th, 1876, contains the following Editorial Notice, which is copied *verbatim et literatum*.

COUNTERFEITING NATURE.

"Mechanics are artisans and ought to be paid in gold," said Ben Johnson, and surely no branch of mechanical art can be better thus defined than that of the manufacturer of artificial limbs upon the most recent and perfected principles. Our attention was called to this subject in such a way as to create a deep interest, thus compelling a searching and thorough investigation, which suprisingly revealed to us the extent of this business. Our surprise at the immense number of cripples was made apparent by facts entirely unknown to us ; such as the war records which figures in round numbers 22,000 cripples among both the blues and grays. This list is much increased by the railroad and innumerable catastrophes to which attention is daily excited through the press. To say in all, A HUNDRED THOUSAND comprising the list, would be approximating below the mark. The causes are numerous and varied, as are the causes of death. Now, why are we so ignorant of this vast catagory of maimed humanity? The question is self-answerable from the standpoints of human nature and the perfection achieved by manufacturers in counterfeiting human members ; human nature will compel a fair young legless damsel to conceal her loss, and would as unhesitatingly deceive others of her actual condition as a man with a glass eye would others of his one-sided observation. If, too, a cripple can conceal his misfortune by the application of a serviceable appendage, money is not spared to meet this end. We felt in our conceit that we knew about all worth knowing concerning artificial limbs, bnt this was cleverly "knocked out" of us by a formal visit to the establishment of probably the largest manufacturer of the United States, if not in the world, that of Mr A. A. Marks, No, 575 Broadway, this City. There we witnessed miracles. Mr. Marks has devoted nearly a quarter of a century to the ameliorating of the condition of the unfortunate crippled world ; a shrewd, keen mechanic, with skill, taste, and ingenuity to back him, he still operates his forces in this subsidiary art.

We witnessed the application of the real article to the patient, and painfully studied his countenance as it changed from that of anticipation to that of realization, or from gloom to joy, and finally to its normal pleasant expression, then came fourth the ejaculation. "*Well, I am again on two legs, as sure as I live, and how strange it seems!*" A second visit to this establishment made us spectators of things stranger than fiction. We were introduced to Mr. John W. January, of Illinois, late corporal Company B, Fourteenth Regiment Illinois Cavalry, a clever-looking fellow, but a subject of two artificial legs. His elastic, lively, and natural step, made us incredulous, but facts revealed themselves, and we listened to the sad story of this late soldier, which we deem worthy of a succinct recital here. We insert it for the edification of the reader.

The regiment in which he held his dignified post was one in that famous Stoneman raid which started from Atlanta with the determination of liberating the prisoners at Andersonville, but which in the attempt was surprised by an overpowering force of the enemy, and he with many others were made prisoners within the very stockade from which they intended to rescue the loyal inmates. He was subsequently transfered to Florence, S. C., while there imprisoned, prostrated by a fever, his feet, by frost, or some unknown cause, literally rotted off. Being sympathized with by four others in a similar manner, the awfulness of his condition was less apparent to himself—all this occurred while Sherman was moving towards the *sea* and up through the State with his invincible force.

Mr. J. informed us that when transfered to our lines he was probably the most emaciated skeleton who ever left the army alive, as he weighed but fifty pounds. He was taken to David's Island with his comrades, and there, particularly through the aid of the Ladies' Union Relief Association, recuperation took place. He told us how he had tried other styles of legs : how he was obliged to discard them and return to his old friend Mr. Marks : how he recovered his health ; the amount of labor he performs (having the care of a large farm in Illinois). He now goes home well equiped for a series of years. We had scarcely aroused ourselves from the silent emotion occasioned by the impressive and heartrending story of Mr. J. when we were introduced to Mr. Frank Stewart, probably the champion on two artificial legs in the world.

A young lady also attracted our attention—sympathy rather—for to consider one of so beautiful and commanding form and captivating demeanor to be destitute of her lower extremities was sad ; but there she was, as fair as a picture just in good condition, favored by age, and a good wooden leg, to claim her amoroso and give her assenting yes to the connubial life. These cases to which our attention was attracted were in the employ of Mr. Marks, who inferred that he gave preference to his subjects, and that others in similar conditions were in his factory.

They practically illustrated the great utility Mr. Marks' substitutes afford the wearers. His labors have not been confined to the United States alone ; in looking over his list, we learn of them being spread far and near, in South and Central America, Europe, and Asia—even in the most remote parts of the earth are to be seen his perambulators. We are assured that he has received most flattering and appreciative letters from his patrons in these parts, which we hope will stimulate him in his future labors for our friends afar off.

PRICES AND TERMS.

For Artificial Legs, applicable to any usual point
of amputation, either above or below knee joint, $100 00

Artificial Arms, for cases where amputation is above
the elbow joint,   -   -   -   -   75 00

Where below, and stump of sufficient length to use
the elbow joint,   -   -   -   50 00

For applying Rubber Feet to other kinds of Legs,
for each foot,   -   -   -   -   -   -   20 00

For applying Rubber Hands to other kinds of Arms,
for each hand,   -   -   -   -   -   -   15 00

For extensions for Legs where shortened by hip
disease or other deformities, also for feet applied in cases of Symes' operations, and also for
parts of hands, the prices have to be arranged
according to the specific cases, after such cases
are clearly understood.

Payment is required with the order, or if the party prefer,
they can pay half in advance, and the balance when the Limb
is completed.

Parties at a distance who object to remitting the whole
amount with the order, and desire their Limbs sent to them
by Express, can pay the balance on delivery of the Limb, provided they will pay the trifling extra expense of collecting.

Being aware that some persons object to thus pay for a
Limb, before receiving it, they should bear in mind that this
is an article made EXPRESSLY to order, and if not taken by
the person for whom it is made, it is a great chance if it fitted
one in a hundred other applicants whom it was not made for.
Thus is readily seen the necessity of advance payment, or part
of it least, at the same time the Patient can rest confident of
just as good a Limb and just as good a fit as they could were
no payment made until after the Limb was delivered, and in
case any mistake or bad fit occurs, the maker holds himself
strictly responsible for any deficiency in this respect caused
by his own or workmen's mistake or carelessness, and will
remedy them without extra charge whenever they occur,
which is very seldom.

Persons coming from a distance, and waiting for their Limbs to be fitted and finished, will receive *particular atten-tion*, and not be detained on expense unnecessarily. Two days is as long as they are generally required to wait, yet sometimes three, but never over that time, unless by some unavoidable and unexpected cause.

HOW TO REMIT.

In making remittances it is preferable to purchase a Draft on some Bank in this City, to my order. If this is not convenient send by Postal Order. Should the amount exceed $50.00 it is necessary to procure more than one, as $50.00 is the largest amount for which an order is issued. Have Postal Orders made payable at Station A, New York City Post Office. Where NEITHER of these facilities can be had, it is best to send the CURRENCY in Registered Letters, which can be done in any Post Office. But for small sums of $5 00 or under it is just as well to send in CURRENCY in an envelope, securely sealed, without registering.

TREATMENT OF STUMPS.

It is very important that the Patient observe great care in treating the stump : move the joints freely to prevent contrac-tion and preserve the natural. motions. Keep it well band-aged from the end upward, in order to reduce and solidify the flesh as much as possible, as it secures a better and much more· perfect fitting Limb, and renders it much more useful and satisfactory, in all respects. Bathing with cold water and vigorous rubbing is also highly beneficial.

DIRECTIONS TO PERSONS WISHING TO PURCHASE LIMBS.

Write me a *full* statement of your case, stating the precise (as near as convenient) point of amputation, whether above or below knee or elbow, condition of stump and time of amputa-tion, and you will receive a blank, giving directions how to take the measures, &c. (free of charge) and any information asked for. This should be done before taking a journey to the manufactory, as in many cases the journey is avoided, by

having the limb fitted from the measures without the party
coming to the manufactory at all, a very desirable consideration to many where means are limited, or the distance far to
travel

Address,

A. A. MARKS,

575 Broadway,

New York City.

CORRESPONDENTS

Are very earnestly requested to be as clear and brief as they
consistently can be in their communications, and also equally
as earnestly desired to write *plain*, and give their address in
full—Town, County, and State.

All communications are answered as prompt as possible.
If no answer is received to letters it must be understood that
either their letters were not received, or that we are unable to
read them, (which is frequently the case).

The amount of labor required in the correspondence alone,
connected with this business, is more than one person ought
to do, and when long and sometimes uninteligible letters, that
an hour's time cannot decipher, with the aid of half a dozen
others, it might as well be admitted that *somebody* is liable
to lose their patience (if they have any), and that *somebody*,
too, may possibly get a short answer, if any.

This is said in all kindness and will not (is trusted) give
any offence, but on the contrary encourage more care in writ-
ing communications, and if in nothing else, thereby save a
great amount of *precious time*.

SOCKS FOR STUMPS.

It is frequently asked by persons in want of Artificial
Limbs (who have not worn them and consequently know but
little about them, or their adjustment) "*Is the socket of the
Artificial Limbs* PADDED, *or what keeps the stump from
coming in contact with the wood, or other hard substance
of the Artificial Limb?*"

In answer to this question you are informed that my
system of shielding and protecting the stump is by using a

neat and well fitting sock, of very fine soft woolen yarn, knit to fit the stump as well as the best fitting stockings or socks do your feet, the sock to extend from the body to end of stump.

I have knitting machines, of the best and most improved kind, constantly at work manufacturing socks, and can furnish them at short notice, to fit any stump, in case they are not among my assortment of some hundreds, constantly kept on hand. One sock is always furnished without charge, with a new Artificial Limb. Orders for any quantity not exceeding four pounds can be sent by mail, to those desiring them.

Seeing the necessity of something of this kind, I adopted this feature of making and supplying these now considered indispensable articles in the year 1868, and it has proved to be quite a business of itself, and of great benefit to those compelled to wear Artificial Limbs.

They are very well adapted to wear on the stump as soon as it is healed, and before applying the Artificial Leg, in order to keep the stump warm and help to compress and strengthen it.

I am prepared to furnish these Socks at the following rates, *wholesale* and *retail*, giving at the same time a system of sizes in accordance with their measurements:

			Price each.	Per doz.
No. 1. For Sock suitable for Stump of 10 inches or less in length, and 15 inches or less in circumference at body, or largest place of measurement,			50 cts.	$5.00
No. 2. " " " over 10 inches	over 15 inches		60 cts.	6.00
No. 3. " " " over 10 inches and not over 15 in length, and 15 in. or less in circum.			60 cts.	6.00
No. 4. " " "	over 15 in circumference,		70 cts.	7.00
No. 5. " " " over 15	over 15 in circumference,	20	70 cts.	7.00
No. 6. " " "	15 or less in		80 cts.	8.00
No. 7. " " " over 20	15 or less "	25	80 cts.	8.00
No. 8. " " "	over 15 "		90 cts.	9.00
No. 9. " " " over 25	15 or less "	30	90 cts.	9.00
No. 10. " " "	over 15 "		$1.00	10.00

½ doz. sold at the same rates as per doz.

In some cases of amputation below knee, a short sock in addition to the full length one is required, to come up only to the knee joint. For such cases, No. 1 or 3 is most suitable.

In taking measures for Socks, please adhere to the following instructions: First, take the length of stump from body to end, inside, then circumference at body and at a distance of about 3 inches apart, in the following manner:

Length of Stump, - - - - - - - - Inches-
Circumference at body. - - - - - - - "
  3 inches from body, - - - - - - "
   " 6 " - - - - - "
   " 9 " - - - - "
   " 12 " - - - "
    &c., &c.

If the measures are from Stump below the knee and to come only to the knee, then commence at knee and state *length from centre of knee joint to end*, circumference at knee, and so on down same as in all other cases. If for knee bearing stump, take measure same as in cases where the knee joint is used and flexible.

Where a single Sock, or less than half a dozen is ordered, the price is at single rates, and sent by mail, at my expense of postage, but where half dozen and upwards are ordered, they are sold at dozen rates, and the purchaser is required to pay the postage in advance, in addition to the price of Socks.

No. 1 Sock weighs 14 to 16 ozs. per doz. No. 5 Sock weighs 26 to 30 ozs. per doz. No. 10 Sock weighs 50 to 64 ozs. per doz.

The postage is two cents every two ozs., and every fraction over. By these figures it is all easily arrived at. The cash must accompany all orders.

ARTIFICIAL LIMBS.

To Commissioned Officers, Soldiers and Seamen of the United States Army and Navy, under new laws and regulations of 1870, 1872 and 1876.

Artificial Limbs have been furnished by the Government to our Nation's Defenders, who suffered amputations, *free of cost to them,* ever since the year 1862. The first law provided but one limb for each amputation; but, in 1870, new laws were passed to supply new limbs, as soon as they could be made, and every *five* years *thereafter.*

In 1872, the law was amended to include as follows: "SHALL APPLY TO ALL OFFICERS, NON COMMISSIONED OFFICERS, ENLISTED AND HIRED MEN OF THE LAND AND NAVAL FORCES OF THE UNITED STATES; WHO, IN THE LINE OF THEIR DUTY AS SUCH, SHALL HAVE LOST OR SUSTAINED BODILY INJURIES, DEPRIVING THEM OF THE USE OF ANY OF THEIR LIMBS, TO BE DETERMINED BY THE SURGEON GENERAL OF THE ARMY.

Section 2.—That the transportation allowed for having Artificial Limbs fitted shall be furnished by the Quartermaster General of the Army.

Section 3.—That the term of FIVE YEARS, specified in the first section of the act approved June 17, 1870, entitled an act to provide for furnishing Artificial Limbs to disabled soldiers, *shall be held to commence in each case with the filing of the application under that act.*"

When fully explained it means *this* :—where the applicants neglect or fail to make their first application under "this law of 1870," that is just so much time lost to them, as their second term commences just *five years* from the date of the receipt and filing of the *first application,* IN THE SURGEON GENERAL'S OFFICE.

All manufacturers of Government Limbs are required to furnish Bonds of two securities of *five thousand dollars each,* for the faithful performance of their work, and the Bonds are required to be renewed every five years.

The following letter from the chief Clerk of the Surgeon General's office explains itself:

War Department, Surgeon General's Office,
Washington, D. C., May 14th, 1875.

Mr. A. A. Marks,

No. 575 Broadway, New York City.

SIR:—I am instructed by the Surgeon General to acknowledge the receipt of your Bond, as a manufacturer of Artificial Limbs for the United States Government, said Bond bearing date May 13th, 1875. It has been examined, found satisfactory and placed on file.

Very respectfully,
Your obedient servent,
SAMUEL RAMSEY,
Chief Clerk.

Having been a Government Manufacturer for so long a term, and also having received a very large portion of the Government orders, especially under the issues of the laws of 1870, the first TWENTY Government orders were in my favor, showing an eagerness of the soldiers to secure my Patent; and ever since then the proportion has continued to increase in my favor, especially in this section, the records show that my Limbs are selected by the soldiers in preference to others. Blanks and instructions complete for filling them up, are sent FREE in all cases to soldiers who wish to apply for Limbs, and also for transportation to come for them, which covers all parts of the United States.

In 1874 Congress passed a law increasing the Pensions of all disabled soldiers whose amputations were AT OR ABOVE THE ELBOW OR AT OR ABOVE THE KNEE OF LEG, to twenty-four dollars per month, in place of eighteen dollars per month as before, PROVIDED that NO Artificial Limb should be furnished to such persons; but this law is now virtually annulled by a recent act which passed just before the close of the first session of the Forty-fourth Congress, and was approved by the President, August 15th, 1876. It reads as follows:

"Be it enacted, etc. : That every Officer, Soldier, Seaman and Marine who, in the line of duty in the Military or Naval Service of the United States, shall have lost a Limb or sustained bodily injury, depriving him of the use of any of his

Limbs, shall receive, once every five years, an Artificial Limb, or appliance therefor, as provided and limited by existing Law, under such regulations as the Surgeon General of the Army may prescribe; and the period of five years shall be held to commence with the filing of the first application, after seventeenth day of June, 1870.

"*Provided,* that this act shall *not* be subject to the proviso of an act entitled '*An Act* to Increase Pensions,' approved June 18, 1874."

It will here be seen that the soldiers and seamen are *all* upon the same footing now, so far as Artificial Limbs are concerned, *without any regard whatever to the rate of pensions, or to the act of June* 18, 1874; and those with amputations at or above knee, elbow, &c., are in the same conditions, as in case no such act had been passed; neither have they lost any time by that act, as their second five years' term will date back to the expiration of the first five years, same as all other cases.

Plain, common sense people select plain and common sense articles. The uncomplicated instruments of war proved the most effectual and most serviceable, and the soldiers know it; and the same rule applies with *equal force* to Artificial Limbs.

My old soldier patrons need no assurance from me now, that they will be fairly dealt with. Those who have no practical knowledge of my limbs or of my reputation as a friend of the soldier, and have no other means of obtaining such knowledge, will do well to correspond with some whose names will be found in the preceding pages of this pamphlet.

ARTIFICIAL LIMBS MADE AND FITTED FROM MEASURES
WITHOUT THE PRESENCE OF THE PATIENT,

Is an important feature to those residing at great distances from the manufactory. It would hardly be expected that persons living in South America, Mexico, Europe, or even our own far off States and Territories, would like to incur the expense of money, time and labor of such a journey, to visit New York City, to obtain my Patent Artificial Limbs; this would in most cases prevent their ever obtaining Limbs at all.

It is already very well known that my Patrons are scattered well over the civilized portions of the world, and too that they do not all come here for their limbs.

Our experience is so extensive in this line, that it will appear to some that there is no necessity of alluding to this subject here, but to others it will be information very gladly received. Among the long list of recommendatory letters from patients, and also the long list of names subscribed to certificate on page 55 of this pamphlet, there is scattered among them many who have thoroughly tested the system of having their limbs fitted from measures. Those cases are marked thus ** as explained on page 35.

Persons desiring further information from those having had the experience will do well to write them upon the subject.

It will be seen that many of them reside but a short distance from the manufactory, or comparatively so, taking into consideration the rapidity and convenience of railroad and steamboat traveling, some under 200 miles.

But let it be clearly understood that it is always preferable to have the patient present to be fitted, and if it suits the convenience of such patient, it is not my business to enquire into the extent of their journey.

Persons ordering limbs to be fitted without their presence, are required to take great care in taking measures. Suitable blanks, with full instructions, are always sent for that purpose. Should errors occur, they are generally discovered upon a thorough examination before the limb is made, and new blanks returned for new measures and drafts, which generally accomplish the desired object. Too much care cannot be had in taking the measures, and they cannot well make mistakes if they adhere *strictly* to the directions that are *plainly* given upon the blank.

There are some cases where amputation is performed at or below ankle-joint, or at wrist in arm, where a plaster cast is needed to insure a good fit ; but these cases are very few (*and ought to be less*) ; but all usual amputations are treated with gratifying success, and at a great saving of time and money to the purchaser.

PRINTED INSTRUCTIONS are always sent with every leg, giving full directions for adjusting the Limb, and treating the stump in all its bearings, which is very important, especially to new beginners.

BRANCHES.

I am frequently asked if I have any Branch at other points, to which the answer *No!* is given.

Convenient and beneficial as it would be in some cases to the patrons, it must be understood that it is not every, even *first class*, workman that is competent to FIT Artificial Limbs as they *ought* to be fitted, *even* with the presence of the patient. Some will make a far better fit with good measures *without* the patient than others will with, and it is just as easy to send measures two or three thousand miles as to send them a short distance, and the cost of Expressing is trifling compared to a journey. It is impossible to have a Branch in every Town, or even every large City, and although I have had in contemplation, and nearly effected arrangements for Branches in several instances, have now fully come to the conclusion to continue to concentrate all my facilities at one point, as the best under all circumstances for my patrons and for myself.

CORK LEGS.

The wonderful power of song has been well exemplified in the old song of the "*Cork Leg.*" When but a mere lad, I remember with striking clearness of going off for a long way through the lonely woods, on a clear autumn night, to visit what is termed in old Connecticut a burning COAL PIT (a process of converting wood into charcoal by fire and heat: the wood is set up in a large pile and covered completely over with turf, then set on fire, and kept burning in a smouldering way for weeks, and requires constant watching day and night.) One of the watchers was a noted song singer, and frequently entertained his nightly visitors with some favorite songs. On that night, among others, he sang the song of the *Cork Leg*, which was then entirely new to me, and made a very lasting impression; indeed, all my way home it kept ringing in my ears how the Cork Leg started off at break-neck speed, taking him with it around the world, as it were, until the poor man was all knocked to pieces, and nothing left but the Cork Leg itself, and that was still going.

Well, I reckon it is going yet, for that old song is still ringing in my ears, and ever since my first entering into this, not exactly "Cork" Leg business, it really seems as if it was continually ringing in everybody else's ears, for hardly a day has passed during the last twenty years but one or more have asked, either by voice or letter, if I made "CORK LEGS," and, although I have answered that question thousands of times, I will here answer and explain, (*I hope* to the satisfaction of all who read the song,) that, although there is sometimes cork used to a very limited extent in the construction of Artificial Legs, and many have said that they had seen legs made of cork *entirely*, yet with a tolerable degree of perseverance I have exercised all the inquisitive powers I have had to spare, either physically or historically, to get hold of a Cork Leg that could be positively located and fastened somewhere ; but ALL my efforts have proved a total failure, and I give up in utter despair of ever finding one single Artificial Leg *made of* CORK. If anybody has one, I should be glad to see it, and would purchase it at a reasonable price, as the most valuable of all my captured trophies of ancient and modern inventions of Artificial Legs. So, here, my friends, you have in this sketch, NOT *what I know about farming*, or what I know about Artificial Legs in general, but what I *do* (and if you please to so consider it), what I DON'T know about *Cork Legs*.

I don't suppose there is anybody living but who has heard of or read this old song, but there may be some yet unborn who will, as a matter of course, be required to get hold of this mythical old invention, so I will here print the *real original* thing itself, that all who read it may know *just exactly* what the Cork Leg is without any mistakes, much as it has amused the youthful ear and enchanted the credulous minds of childhood in listening to the songster's vivid portrayal of the Cork Leg, thereby entertaining in a measure the whole world ; (or, at least, I have good reason to think so, for I have never conversed with any one on the Cork Leg subject that has not either heard it sung or talked about in some way). In this way it has done some good, but in another direction it has done mischief, for many unthinking, unlucky ones have been wofully disappointed by anticipations created in the Cork Leg song (*fabulous and unreasonable as it is*), as they really supposed it would not only get up and walk off itself, but would take them along with it, without an effort of their own.

Should this have the effect to, in a reasonable degree, satisfy those enquiries about Cork Legs, and at the same time dispel the false illusions heretofore created in the imaginary minds of many, the object of this explanation will be accomplished.

THE CORK LEG.

I

I'll tell you a tale now without any flam,
 In Holland there dwelt Mynheer Von Clam,
Who every morning said, "I am
 The richest merchant in Rotterdam."
  Ri tu, di nu, di nu, di nu,
  Ri tu, di ni nu, ri tu, di nu, ri na.

II.

One day, when he had stuff'd him as full as an egg,
 A poor relation came to beg:
But he kick'd him out without broaching a keg,
 And in kicking him out he broke his leg.
  Ri tu, di nu, etc.

III.

A surgeon, the first in his vocation,
 Came and made a long oration:
He wanted a limb for anatomization,
 So he finished his jaw by amputation.
  Ri tu, di nu, etc.

IV.

"Mr. Doctor," says he, when he'd done his work,
 "By your sharp knife I lose one fork:
But on two crutches I never will stalk,
 For I'll have a beautiful leg of cork."
  Ri tu, di nu, etc.

V.

An Artist in Rotterdam 'twould seem,
 Had made cork legs his study and theme;
Each joint was as strong as an iron beam,
 And the springs were a compound of clock-work and steam.
  Ri tu, di nu, etc.

VI.

The leg was made, and fitted right;
    Inspection the Artist did invite ;
Its fine shape gave Mynheer delight,
        As he fixed it on and screw'd it tight.
            Ri tu, di nu, *etc.*

VII.

He walk'd thro' squares and pass'd each shop ;
    Of speed he went to the utmost top;
Each step he took with a bound and a hop,
        And he found his leg he could not stop !
            Ri tu, di nu, *etc.*

VIII.

Horror and fright were in his face !
    The neighbors tho't he was running a race ;
He clung to a lamp-post to stop his pace,
        But the leg wouldn't stay, but kept on the chase.
            Ri tu, di nu, *etc.*

IX.

Then he call'd to some men with all his might,
    "Oh ! stop this leg, or I'm murder'd quite !"
But, though they heard him aid invite,
        In less than a minute he was out of sight.
            Ri tu, di nu, *etc.*

X.

He ran o'er hill and dale and plain,
    To ease his weary bones he'd fain ;
Did throw himself down, but all in vain—
        The leg got up, and was off again.
            Ri tu, di nu, *etc.*

XI.

He walk'd of days and nights a score ;
    Of Europe he had made the tour :
He died—but though he was no more,
        The leg walk'd on the same as before !
            Ri tu, di nu, *etc.*

.